ANANSESEM

ANANSESEM

Telling Stories and
Storytelling African Maternal Pedagogies

Adwoa Ntozake Onuora

DEMETER PRESS, BRADFORD, ON

The publisher gratefully acknowledges the the financial assistance of the Government of Canada through the Canada Book Fund.

Canadä

Demeter Press
140 Holland Street West
P. O. Box 13022
Bradford, ON L3Z 2Y5
Tel: (905) 775-9089
Email: info@demeterpress.org
Website: www.demeterpress.org

Demeter Press logo based on the sculpture "Demeter" by Maria-Luise Bodirsky <www.keramik-atelier.bodirsky.de>

Printed and Bound in Canada

Library and Archives Canada Cataloguing in Publication

Onuora, Adwoa Ntozake, 1982–, author
        Anansesem : telling stories and storytelling African maternal pedagogies / Adwoa Ntozake Onuora.

Includes bibliographical references.
ISBN 978-1-927335-19-2 (paperback)

        1. Storytelling. 2. Discourse analysis, Narrative. 3. Education--Biographical methods. 4. Autobiography--Authorship. 5. Motherhood.
I. Title.

GR72.3.O58 2015   808.5'43   C2015-901650-9

To Ma'at,
for liberating me

Contents

Acknowledgements

AFRICAN AMERICAN FEMINIST INTELLECTUAL bell hooks was apt in her assessment when she stated that, "it is not easy to name our pain, to make it a location of theorizing" (1994, p.74). The chartering of this new theoretical trajectory on African maternal pedagogies, like the birth of my daughter, was without a doubt one of the most difficult and painful journeys of my life. However, like Ma'at's birthing, the journey culminated into this moment—a moment of inexplicable joy—where I am finally able to hold the fruit of a labour of love against my bare bosom, tears flowing from the depths of my soul, because she is finally here—complete, whole, real.

I did not labour alone. While enduring the labour pains, I held firmly to the hands of living theorists who embody bravery, resistance, hope and love. I am eternally grateful to my learning community—African mothers and community/othermothers who "courageously exposed their wounds" (hooks, 1994, p. 74) and shared with me the memories of their lived experiences so that I could create stories that add to theory-building about the value of African women's maternal teachings. To Dr. Gary Knowles, thank you for being my epidural when I dashed all hope of being able to ride the waves of pain to the end. Thank you for your patience, wisdom, creative insights and for your constant reminders to trust the process. I am extremely proud of this beautiful scholartistry. I would also like to thank Dr. Rita Deverell, Dr. Jean-Paul Restoule and Dr. June Larkin for their overwhelmingly positive feedback.

I am extremely grateful to Dr. George J.S Dei for his critical insight and support when I started out as a Master's student at OISE. You provided me with a strong theoretical grounding that I will carry with me throughout my academic career. Dr. Njoki Wane, thank you for introducing me to Black Feminist Thought. And, Dr. Andrea O'Reilly, I am so appreciative of your theorizing, skill, patience, commitment and hard work in keeping MIRCI alive. Your very high degree of knowledge of the scholarship on maternal theory contributed to my being able to feel more confident in the merits of committing our stories on mothering to paper.

I am thankful to my first teacher, my mother, Winsome Williamson, for holidays spent with her that filled my childhood with so many colourful memories and lessons. And to my father, Garfield Reddie, thank you for instilling in me the value of hard work and dedication. In my darkest hours I found my way back to these teachings and drew on them for sustenance.

I am also deeply grateful to Ricardo Martin, affectionately called "Uncle Ricky," Imara Rolston, Rebecca Price, Makesha Roberts, Ajamu Nangwaya, Carol-Lynne D'Arcangelis, Ijeoma Ekoh, Julie Oulette, Devi, Mandeep, Kumalo and Nandi Mucina. Thank you all for your constant love, guidance, support and for helping me raise Ma'at while on this journey. It definitely takes a village!

I must also acknowledge the community of scholars at OISE: Paul Adjei, Arlo Kempf, Michelle Bailey, Stanley Doyle-Wood, Everton Cummings, and Selena Nemorin for their critical feedback and advice at different points of the writing process. To Ajamu, thank you for the many challenging questions which sent me back to the drawing board. I am most grateful for your friendship while navigating the alienating Ivory Towers of the academy. Thank you Jacqui Terry (illustrator extraordinaire) for your creative expertise, hard work and technical skills in making what was a mere vision, an aesthetic treat. Thanks are also due to Sangsters' Book Store for granting me the permission to use the iconic storytelling reproductions of the late Honorable Louis Bennett Coverly. Big ups to

Joan Grant-Cummings for your support, mentorship, sistahood and for your feedback.

Segments of Chapter 4 and 5 have been previously published in my articles "Killing Me Softly: On Mother Daughter Resistance," *Canadian Woman Studies/les cahiers de la femme*'s issue on "Women Writing 4" 30.1 (2013) and "I Feel Therefore I Can Be/long: Cultural Bearing as Maternal Activism," *Journal of Motherhood Initiative for Research and Community Involvement* 3.2 (2012). The Epilogue, has also appeared in my article "HERstory is OURstory: An Afro-indigenous Response to the Call for "Truth" in Narrative Representation, *Cultural Studies <=> Critical Methodologies* 13.5 (2013). I would like to thank the editorial board of these journals for their insights and critical feedback that helped me to develop my ideas. I am grateful for the space these journals provided for me to publish my work.

And finally, to my womb blessing Ma'at, thank you for choosing me. You were my constant company, my muse, my motivation who made your presence known through nights of relentless gymnastics in my stomach as I trudged through the mess of course work and writing. We journeyed this road together. Only strangely enough, it was you carrying me all this time.

Prologue

The bath water is hot.
I resist being lulled to sleep by the aroma of lavender-scented incense infused with quiet notes of peppermint oil.
With each exhale, fog droplets ascend, coating the bathroom mirror.
I lie on my back, water covers all but my protruding stomach.
Blissful, I bask in the last few moments of 'me time'.
I imagine what it will be like when she arrives.
No more silence perhaps?
I think that I will soon have to surrender what was once my time to the being I carry in my womb.
I embrace the deafening silence, waiting for the lesson that it brings, realizing that there will be fewer of these in the years to come.
My body grows weary.
I close my eyes and am carried away.
I remember.

GROWING UP IN JAMAICA, I was fed a rich diet of Big Boy and Anancy stories. Neighbourhood children regaled each other with folktales shrouded in language that craftily masked curse words and facilitated playful exploration of taboo subject matters. To me, Big Boy and Anancy stories were a source of entertainment and hilarity. But there were other stories. Stories told by adults couched in proverbs and sayings. Stories imbued with both literal and symbolic meaning. Stories that relayed important information about our values and beliefs. These were the stories women shared as they gathered in hair salons, prepared elaborate feasts in kitchens or laboured over piles of laundry on washdays. These were their personal stories—the stories that helped them cope with various issues as they negotiated relationships and life.

The practice of storytelling is common throughout various indigenous communities across the globe. Among African people, stories serve as an important medium for the articulation of culture, history and ancestral memory. Storytelling is an important tool for the celebration and reclamation of African heritage. To date, storytelling continues to serve as platform for resisting neo-colonialism and various forms of social oppression (Banks-Wallace, 1998; Pedraill, 2007; Marshall, 2006; 2007; 2008). The writings of critical race theorists (Bell, 1987; Collins, 1998; Crenshaw, Gotanda, Peller & Thomas 1995; Delgado, 1989, 1995; Lorde, 1984; Matsuda, 1996; Parker, Dehyle, Villennas & Nebecker, 1998; Soloranzo, 1998; Williams, 1991; Wing, 1997) affirm the socio-political significance of storytelling to oppressed peoples.

Within the North American context where African people continue to face multiple and intersecting forms of oppression, our stories become particularly important because as Dalia Rodriquez explains, they function as a means of psychic self-preservation, offering an outlet for healing from our wounds. Citing Delgado (1989) and Freire (1970), Rodriquez (2006) asserts that our stories are critical to the extent that they "illuminate the material and social conditions that provide a means to usher in social change" (p. 1068). Despite these scholars theorizing on the significance of storytelling for the oppressed, our stories remain marginalized and devalued within formal spaces of learning. Often rooted in oral literary traditions, indigenous storytelling is either dismissed or subject to credibility tests by so-called experts. Notwithstanding these challenges, marginalized people continue to give voice to our stories. As researchers within the academy, we continue to use our stories as spaces from which to enact resistance (hooks, 1990), engage in meaning making and "assert our subjectivities as creators, theorists and interpreters of texts" (Lawrence, 1995 as cited in Rodriguez, 2010, p. 494).

So, what makes a story a story? Is storytelling simply a narration of experience? Do cultural stories differ from everyday narrations of experience or self/personal stories? These are some key questions that I think warrant clarification before I lay out how it is that I came to writing this composite story.

In thinking through the above questions, Banks-Wallace (1998) offers the following conceptual framework:

> A story is an event or series of events, encompassed by temporal or spatial boundaries, that are shared with others using an oral medium or sign language. Storytelling is the process of interaction used to share stories. People sharing a story (storytellers) and those listening to a story (storytakers) are the main elements of story telling. (p.17)

Within this framework, we can extend our conceptual understanding by thinking of stories as constituting three different modes: i) metanarratives of cultural groups ii) personal/self stories and iii) cultural stories. The first type—metanarratives— serve to tell a larger story about a people. For example, the story of Africans in the Diaspora typifies a story about a larger story—a story of Africans as an ethno-cultural group. Another example is the dominant cultural story that reinforces the idea of European 'superiority' in relation to racialized groups of people (Delgado, 1989). We can therefore view such stories as a large fabric, and each of our individual personal stories, our folklore, proverbs, parables and sayings, as tiny threads interwoven through this larger piece of fabric. The result is a work of art that distills a people's ideas on morals, ethics, social knowledges and cultural identities.

The second type—self or personal stories—are narrations of a series of events that an individual or individuals (within a given cultural group) experience. These include poems, fictional novels, autoethnographies, autobiographies and memoirs (Denzin, 1997; Ellis & Bochner, 2006). Personal narratives Rodriguez (2009) tells us allow the individual to become both the subject and object of study in the examination of social phenomena. The third—cultural stories—I conceive of as falling within the category of folklore, proverbs, sayings, parables, music and other oral literary mediums.

Whereas narratives of the self may or may not have symbolic significance, cultural stories carry the folk philosophies of a people and have deeply embedded symbolic meaning(s) and significance beyond their literal meaning. Anancy folktales are an example of a cultural story. Moreover, what sets cultural stories apart from those previously mentioned is that they are embodied performance arts requiring dramatization and mastery of cultural languages (Mello, 2001). This is why in Afro-indigenous societies in particular, when collectors of folklore enter these communities, they are directed to a chief storyteller who the community has named as the person versed at distilling these types of stories.

Take for example the Jamaican Anancy stories told by the late iconic folklorist the Honorable Louise Bennett-Coverly. These stories have been in the public domain in parts of the Caribbean and the Americas having travelled with enslaved Africans along the Trans-Atlantic. Anancy stories are part of the historical memory of formerly enslaved Africans brought to the 'new world'. Although the stories have been retold by Jamaicans throughout the generations, they have for the most part been associated with the Honorable Louise Bennett-Coverly. This is so even though we know that the Jamaicanized version of the Akan Anancy stories are not owned by any particular individual, but instead belong to Africans and the African Diaspora community.

This begs the question: What then sets the Honorable Loise Bennett-Coverly apart from others as chief storyteller of Anancy folktales? She was especially gifted with the ability to narrate the Anancy stories with dramatization and mimicry steeped in the vernacular of the Jamaican people. Moreover, she possessed the capacity to playfully manipulate the language in a way that captivated audiences of all ages. Today, even in her passing, she is hailed as one of Jamaica's chief folklorists. From this we see that in Afro-indigenous communities, the storyteller is a socially sanctioned role. While anyone can narrate their personal experience (which then forms part of the larger story of a cultural group), not just anyone can be a teller of cultural stories. Additionally, not every narration of one's personal experience (because of the element of symbolism) can be viewed as a cultural story.

Saying that does not however negate the fact that an individual's personal story could become institutionalized as cultural memory to the extent of becoming folklore. Nelson Mandela's life story for instance, serves as part of a larger cultural story that testifies to the indomitable spirit of African peoples. Mandela's story when located within the broader historical and social context of anti-colonialism, becomes more than a narration of events in his life. His is a story that, because of the interrelated conditions at the time has deeper symbolic meaning(s), and therefore serves a larger purpose. My point here is that narrations of the self, left uncontextualized, do not necessarily amount to a cultural story. They remain simply oral or literary text without context (Dundee, 1966).

So how did I come to writing this narrative representation on African women's maternal pedagogies? Well, the catalyst for this storied remembering emerged from self-reflections on my journey to biological motherhood. As I became visibly pregnant, I began experiencing readings of my body that constantly reminded me of my "M(other)" status within various spaces. I was puzzled by the occasions when suitemates would express passive aggressive behaviour towards me, infuriated by a clerk's asking while I waited outside my dorm one morning "Are you waiting for your baby daddy?", saddened when physicians who, having never met my partner at pre-natal check ups, felt comfortable enough voicing "concerns" about his whereabouts, and disheartened when I walked the halls of my department—the one space I naively thought was free of judgment—and was met with the occasional disappointing eyes.

During this time, I was mid-way through a graduate seminar entitled "Black Feminist Thought" where I became exposed to a small sampling of literature on the subject of African women and mothering. I found solace in the works of African feminist writers like Stanlie M. James, Patricia Bell-Scott (1993), Patricia Hill-Collins (1986, 1987, 2000a, 2000b), bell hooks (1981, 2000, 2007, 2007b), and Audre Lorde (1982, 1997, 2007) who reminded me that I was not alone. I realized then that African women had been resisting and learning how to navigate the spoken and unspoken poetics of racism that reconstituted us as always and already "mammies," "jezebels," and "welfare queens," who to paraphrase Jenkins (1998), "emasculated our sons and defeminized our daughters" (p. 204). Inspired by their ideas I thought: What better way to rupture the established knowledge (both inside and outside the academy) than to pursue research that would continue this legacy of counter-storytelling (Delgado, 1989; Soloranzo, 1998; Soloranzo & Yasso, 2002) in the context of mothering? The weaving of Anancy stories into our personal stories of African mothering is foundational to continuing this tradition of resistance through reclamation of African ways of knowing.

In the fall of 2008, after giving birth to my daughter (and in preparation for the writing of my comprehensive examination), I scoured the University catalogue for resources on African women and motherhood. Not only did I find literature on African women's diverse experiences of mothering, I was relieved to discover a research centre (the Association of Research on Motherhood/ ARM, now the Motherhood Initiative for Community and Research Involvement/MIRCI) that housed a growing body of literature exploring various aspects of mothering from diverse subject locations. MIRCI provided an outlet for the voices of activists, scholars, and academics of all genders, cultures and social locations who had an interest in theorizing and developing scholarship on motherhood.

This storied account is influenced by feminist scholarship on mothering, motherhood, maternal theory and maternal thinking that I have over the years come across. It is informed by the works of theorists such as Sara Ruddick (1989), Adrienne Rich (1986), Valerie Walkerdine and Helen Lucy (1989), Fiona Joy Green (2004, 2006) and Andrea O'Reilly (1998, 2000, 2004a, 2004b, 2004c, 2006, 2007a, 2007b. 2008, 2009a, 2009b) whose ideas paved the way for more complex readings of motherhood that challenged earlier feminist paradigms where motherhood was seen as an automatically patriarchal and oppressive space. It was their (re)visioning of mothering and motherwork as a female defined site that could potentially afford women agency and power that propelled me to continue my quest for works that spoke to how I too could practice empowered mothering.

Although I utilize the ideas of these theorists, it was the African feminists maternal theorists who "peopled the writing" (Morrison, 1981, p. xiv) of the stories you are about to read. Their interpretations and perspectives resonated more with me because of my own personal location as an Afro-Jamaican woman, daughter and mother. At another equally important level, I had made it my political and academic project to center voices such as ours that are traditionally silenced in mainstream discourses. Worth noting are the writings of African women like Patricia Hill-Collins (1987, 1991, 1994, 2000b), Stanlie James (1994), Njoki Wane (2000) and Arlene Edwards (2000) who not only cemented ideas that mothering has and continues to be a site of empowerment, resistance and agency (particularly for African women and the children they mother), but also ruptured the Eurocentric, patriarchal and gendered conceptualizations of motherhood. I found the ideas espoused in theirs and other writings of African women in journals such as *Jenda: Journal of Culture and African Women's Studies*, particularly useful in terms of providing alternative readings of motherhood that extended beyond the male/female binary and the Western nuclear family model. These writings illuminated a long-standing African centred tradition of "mothering" through the phenomenon of kinship networks and community/othermothering (see also the works of Nzegwu, 2005, 2006; Oyewumi, 2000, 2003a, 2003b; Rabenoro, 2003; Sudarksa, 2005 for more extensive discussions on the concept of community/othermothering in parts of the African continent). For me—a child of the eighties, having experienced this "it takes a village to raise a child" model in the context of the Caribbean where it was still valued—reading the works of African women who theorized about mothering through this prism was familiar and comforting.

The stories are also shaped by the constellation of African maternal thinkers whose writings explore the interconnection between the scholarly and motherly work of African women (Bernard & Bernard, 1998; Bernard et al., 2000; Mogadime, 1998; Perryman-Mark, 2000; Thomas, 2000) as well as those that connect motherwork to identity formation (Mackey, 2000), and examined African women's mothering and activism (James, 1994), African women's mothering at the intersection of spirituality (Duncan, 2005) and writings that focused on the symbolic and literal representations of African mothers in mediums such as cinema (Duncan, 2005) and literature (Anatol, 2002; Lawson, 2000; Patton, 2000; Steele, 2000, Willey, 2000). Later, as I began to learn and develop creative writing skills through writing courses, I immersed myself in the works of African women writers who used the framework of the creative imagination to theorize about the literal and symbolic significance of African women as mothers and community/othermothers (Kincaid, 1985, 1997, 1998; Hartman, 2007; hooks, 1992; Morrison, 1981, 1998, 2000).

Even as became exposed to these creative and academic perspectives on African mothering, I felt that very few works explored the link between mothering and teaching. With the exception of Andrea O'Reilly who had already begun writing on African women, cultural bearing and the motherline, and scholars like Fiona Joy Green, Deborah Lea Byrd and Dolana Mogadime who made connections between mothering and critical and feminist pedagogies, I had not come across (at the time) literary or scholarly writings that dealt directly and at great length with the learning associated with and influenced by women of African descent who engaged in the practice of mothering. As an educational researcher, this was a critical gap that piqued my interest. I began to think critically about the possibilities of marrying feminist pedagogies with the motherwork of African women and decided much later that storytelling would be the form through which I would engage with and theorize about the learning that took place while African women engaged in what Sara Ruddick calls maternal practice and thought.

Anansesem: Telling Stories and Storytelling African Maternal Pedagogies is a metanarrative that uses personal and cultural stories to focus on the contemporary realities and complexities of African women's maternal practices—described as the work that mothers engage in when they set out to fulfill the demands of motherwork (that is, nurturing, protection, training and cultural bearing) and their maternal thinking—the specific discipline of thought, a cluster of attitudes, beliefs and values that arise out of engaging in motherwork (O'Reilly, 2004; Ruddick, 1989). The book focuses then on how women of African descent through a combination of maternal practice and maternal thinking produce maternal pedagogies.

Before walking you through the general framework and interrelated issues that shaped these stories, I want to first explore the meaning of maternal pedagogies (or mothering as pedagogy) as spoken about by Fiona Joy Green. In *Feminist Mothering in Theory and Practice 1985-1995*, Green describes feminist pedagogies as "the art, science and/or act of teaching that one engages in through motherwork and that is un/consciously informed by a critical feminist consciousness, that challenges all forms of oppressions and is geared toward social change and equity" (2011, p. 198).

In thinking about feminist pedagogies as necessarily encompassing an intersectional approach that challenges the varying manifestations of oppression, Green's work touches on an issue not taken up in Rich's (1986) groundbreaking work *Of Woman Born*, where she distinguishes between mothering as experience (a female defined site that can be potentially empowering) and institution (a male defined site of women's oppression). In theorizing about how motherhood is both an institution and experience, Rich does not address how even within this patriarchally governed institution of motherhood, all mothers are not created equal. In other words, some women are not accorded the status of mothers, and are therefore not extended the 'courtesy' of having their mothering scrutinized through this patriarchal institution in the first place. With that said, a key illuminating idea for me in Green's examination of the relationship between feminist mothering practice and pedagogy is her acknowledgement that the feminist mother and educator (because of their different experiences) work differently across different contexts. As such, they necessarily employ different pedagogical tools as they teach children to be critically conscious of and challenge various forms of oppression that intersect and interlock to maintain the larger patriarchal matrix of domination (Green, 2008, 2011).

Adding to hers and previous motherhood scholars who examined the interconnection between maternal thinking and feminist maternal pedagogies (Ruddick, 1989; O'Reilly and Ruddick, 2009; Green, 2003) I use race based theories (specifically African centred feminism(s), Indigeneity and Afrocentricity) to examine the specific contexts and experiences of the feminist maternal pedagogies of mothering peoples of African descent. These frameworks become particularly useful in analyzing how African women practice feminist pedagogies within the context of their culturally defined feminist mothering. This book contributes in a new way to motherhood scholarship in that it provides (using the medium of stories) real life examples of how maternal pedagogies work in general and more specifically some of the characteristics and expressions of maternal pedagogies rooted in and informed by African cultural traditions, experiences and worldviews.

Even as the research text uses the framework of the creative imagination, it is important that you the reader see them as more than just fictional recreations. The following quote by Toni Morrison on the use of fiction serves to stem such impulses. She explains:

> [The writer's] job becomes how to rip that veil drawn over "proceedings too terrible to relate." The exercise is also critical for any person who is [African], or who belongs to any marginalized category, for historically, we were seldom invited to participate in the discourse even when we were its topic. Moving that veil aside requires, therefore, certain things. First of all, I must trust my own recollections. I must also depend on the recollections of others. *Thus, memory weighs heavy in what I write, in how I begin and in what I find to be significant.* But memories and recollections won't give me access to the unwritten interior life of these people. *Only the act of the imagination can help me....* No matter how "fictional" the account of ... writers, or how much it was a product of invention, *the act of imagination is bound up with memory ... remembering where you used to be.... It is emotional memory ...* [w]hat makes it fiction is the nature of the imaginative act: my reliance on the image—on the remains—in addition to recollection to yield up a kind of truth (Morrison, 1987, pp. 111-119, emphasis added).

Morrison's ideas are illuminating in terms of reinforcing the theoretical significance of creative non/fiction and art in general. Because I toy with imaginings to present to you a "story within another" (Walkerdine, 1989, p. 2), I am cognizant of the potential for audiences to view these stories as "make belief." With that in mind, I would say that these stories originate from African women's individual and collective memories of living in a context where a larger (though fictional) cultural story dominates. This dominant (also imagined) story continues to overshadow our experiences of resisting and navigating negative stereotypes. Therefore as Morrison suggests, the act of storying, of imagination is inextricably connected to our emotional memories and by extension our lived realities. It is connected to our experiences living in a space where we are silenced, where primacy is given to empiricism, objectivism and positivism, and where the stories of African mothers (biological or social), our multiple subjectivities and ways of knowing are subjugated (Matsuda, 1989; Razack, 1993).

The book thus starts from a place of recognizing that as Afro-indigenous people in general, and as African women who mother in a highly racist, sexist, classist, homophobic and ableist context, our stories have been taken, appropriated and misused. More importantly, because "the Western academy has denied our intellectual agency" (Dei, 2006, p. 4), I use our stories to transform ideas about what is considered valid knowledge. Telling multiple stories about African women who use mothering as a site of empowerment is my attempt at presenting counter-stories (Delgado, 1989) rooted in African conceptualizations of mothering that dislodges the dominant Eurocentric narrative.

The stories' framework holds firstly that the African mother is an important site of cultural retention. As creators of knowledge, African mothers and community/othermothers are actively engaged in challenging the epistemological inequities of a Eurocentric master narrative. Secondly, that personal and cultural stories, when placed within the broader socio-political context of systemic whiteness, become vitally important in theorizing about collective, self-knowledge and the empowerment of African peoples. Finally, the stories attest to how empowered feminist maternal pedagogies are both modeled and taught (O'Reilly, 2008). They reinforce the idea that African mothers and community/othermothers through feminist maternal pedagogies informed by cultural consciousness, become central to the African child's social, identity, educational development and survival.

The stories represent a fusion of what Sbrocchi (2008) calls collective rememberances about the struggles and joys that accompany African-Canadian women's motherwork. They are inspired by and based on conversations I had with eight women identified persons of African descent living in Toronto, Canada. In my initial narrative inquiry, the women were asked to speak on their conceptions of mothering as well as their perceptions of their role as mothers, changes in their experiences of being mothered compared to their own mothering practices, the effects of social identity markers and social location on these changes, and whether they conceived of themselves as key cultural bearers or educators for African-Canadian children. I later transcribed our conversations and organized our shared stories around substantive themes consistent with the findings of current feminist research on motherhood, African centred feminism(s) and indigenous theorizing.

Our conversations are (re)presented through creative non-fictional stories on the themes of i) cultural bearing, spirituality and the motherline ii) conceptions of mothering iii) surviving, negotiating and (strategically) surrendering to individual, cultural, institutionalized and systemic forms of racism iv) resistance to the master narrative as well as hegemonic and normalizing tendencies of society and v) the consequences of African women's culturally defined feminist mothering and maternal pedagogies.

This book is an offering to you of a creative and emotionally engaging alternative for representing contemporary educational research. Using arts-informed narrative representation—that is, research whose primary empirical data is informed by the literary genre and comprised of self/personal narration, cultural stories, and illustrations, I engage in what Toni Morrison calls "literary archaeology" (1987, p.112). Each chapter in this collection of storied rememberances represents my getting at some essence of salient themes that came out of the research. Consistent with Morrison's framework on using the creative imagination to present lived experiences, I draw on information from my co-participants transcripts, engage in reconstruction of key moments, in order to take you on an exciting narrative journey through our lives recalled from our emotional memories.

Note to Readers

I LIKE TO THINK THAT THIS BOOK has a little bit of something for everyone. After all, one of the broad goals of arts-informed research is to make scholarship more accessible in a way that connects with wide and diverse audiences (Cole & Knowles, 2000, 2008). For the everyday reader who picks up this book, you may want to immerse yourself in the first section that entails the five storied chapters. If you choose to start there, you will notice that there are multiple layers embedded within the storied text.

The first layer or main body of text consists of storied memories re-created from transcribed conversations with the women on their lived experiences and practices of mothering. Here, you will also access my personal stories of being a recipient of African women's mothering and community/othermothering. Frequently, these are punctuated by stories where I am engaged in nurturance, mother-work, and cultural bearing with my daughter Ma'at through the practice of Anancy folk storytelling. This approach of intertwining multilayered stories is inspired by Susan Sbrocchi's methodological approach—one that evidences the process of theorizing and making knowledge claims from stories. She explains:

> To be able to listen for the story the other person is telling I need to know my own story. I need to see where the line of my story takes a pause, intersects, and deviates from their stories. I need to be able to see the sketched lines of their lives in this place. The strength of their reflexive process is depicted in the fusion of collective remembrances and,

although, the sketchy line that becomes the central organizing construct are the lines of my life, the representation
of the interconnection of our shared experiences is crucial
to the rigorous quality [and educative possibilities] of the
work. (2008, p. 204)

Consistent with this approach, this layered storied form represents
my attempt at sketching lines that facilitate the type of self-reflex-
ivity that the arts-informed researcher necessarily undergoes in the
process of meaning making (Cole & Knowles, 2008). Through it,
I am able then to pinpoint the convergences and divergences in our
larger collective stories on African maternal pedagogies.

Throughout the book, I also use endnotes as an additional layer
of text to: i) expand on my thoughts external to the main narrative
ii) give conceptual clarity and expand on terminologies iii) provide
English translations to the Jamaican language and iv) connect
the storied memories to theories of African centred feminism(s),
maternal theory, and indiginiety.

For readers schooled in the language of the academy, you might
want to begin by reading the prologue. Here I lay out the central
thesis, intent and impetus for the storied account. Here, I also begin to discuss key concepts and methodological issues, questions
and challenges. If you have not sufficiently wet your palate after
reading the prologue, you may want to delve right into the epilogue. Again, here you will find a storied dialogue between myself
and one of my co-participants where we attempt to expose some
of the methodological and ethical challenges, power relations as
well as provide further framing and context for other conceptual
and theoretical issues that underlie the work.

A key thing to note here is that this section is my attempt at
fusing the language of traditional social science with the languages, processes, and forms of the literary art form that inspires,
frames and defines the research inquiry process (Cole & Knowles,
2000). The representational form—that is my choosing to story
the methodological and theoretical framework for the personal
and cultural stories—is purposeful, meant to give consistency to
the chosen art form. This move is also consistent with the broad
agenda of arts-informed inquiry with its expressed goal to inject

life into what I feel would have otherwise been a section written in language "wrung dry of emotion, of sensuality, of physicality [and humanness]" (Cole & Knowles, 2000, p. 57). The goal here is to enhance the readers' understanding—in an accessible and engaging manner—of the phenomenon of maternal pedagogies as viewed through the prism of African women's maternal identity.

In the preceding paragraphs, I have offered a general guide that I hope will better orient you as you journey through this book. However, understand that this is only a guide. So, when you read, please feel free to charter your own course. On a final note, in anticipation that you may wonder: How is this scholarship? Can stories advance knowledge especially when they arise from what is often construed as "fictional" representations? Though these questions are valid and warrant some attention, be forewarned that it is not intended to reflect how we actually experience and process the world around us (Cole & Knowles, 2000, p. 59). Having said this, I ask that you enter these stories with an understanding that they are my creative interpretations taken from my fragmented memories, stitched together with the memories of the experiences of eight other women. Of course, there are other interpretations possible. With this in mind, I invite you to offer up your own (creative) interpretations or better yet, tell other stories on African women's maternal pedagogies.

Chapter 1.
Pedagogies of the Spirit

The Crossing:Anancy Encounters Nyame the Sky God
Jacqui Terry, © Images Copyright 2012 (used with permission) www.jacquiterry.com.

Tell Me a Story

"ONE MORE STORY PLEASE, please Mummy?" Ma'at's small beady eyes glisten, she smiles knowing that I will give in.

"Alright, alright," I say. "But after this one it's time to go to sleep." Her eyes glean with excitement. We lay close in the night, buried under the fluffy white cotton duvet. She stares out at me in anticipation, waiting for me to tell her a new tale.

"This is the story of *How Anancy came from Afrika to the Americas*."[1]

Looking down at her I ask, "Can you say Afrika?" I hear her not-yet-three-year-old voice clumsily utter "Afr-ee-eka."

"Not bad for a first try kiddo," I say giggling.

She smiles pleasingly and repeats "Afr-ee-ka" twice more.

"Afrika is a beautiful place where all the dark skinned people of the world like you and me come from."

She listens, moves in closer and nestles her face deeper into my chest. My heart beats passionately against the side of her cheek.

"Well, that is where Anancy is from," I continue. I hear my voice pierce the quiet black night as I begin to string together from memory words that tell a story of how we got to this place.

*

A long time ago Anancy lived in a village in the Kingdom of Asante.[2] One morning, before the cock crowed, Anancy picked up his machete and spear and went into the bushes. He walked for miles and miles until he came upon some fresh tracks of a warthog. Anancy was a very curious little spider, so he decided he would follow the tracks deep into the grassland. Some time later, he stumbled upon more tracks. Anancy was smart. He knew by the shape of the imprints left in the dirt that the warthog mustn't be too far away.

His mouth began to water and his stomach growled. GRRR! He dreamt of sinking his teeth into juicy roasted warthog meat.

Upon reaching a patch of tall grass, Anancy saw the warthog lying on its side. Someone else had killed it. "What is this I see?" Anancy asked himself. "A dead warthog and no one here to claim it! Ah, I wonder who was so kind enough to leave this meat here for me?" Anancy scratched his head and thought and thought.

"Oh, I know," he exclaimed rubbing his hands together. "It must be Nyame the Sky God. Nyame must have seen that I was tired and hungry, he took pity on me and struck the beast down with lightening so that I would not have to do the hard work of killing it myself. I must thank Nyame."

He quickly picked up some dry sticks, made a fire and mounted the warthog on a wooden pole over the flames. Soon the warthog was roasting. But before the roasted meat had time to cool, and without giving thanks to Nyame, Anancy quickly devoured it. He ate and ate until there was nothing left but a piece of the warthog's foot.

Suddenly, Osebo the Leopard appeared out of the bushes carrying some firewood, a large drinking gourd filled with water, and a cooking pot. He looked around for the warthog he had killed, but it had vanished. All Osebo saw in its place was Anancy the spider, lying asleep, his stomach stuffed with a pleasing smile on his face.

He then realized what had happened. Anancy had eaten all the warthog meat by himself. Osebo became so angry he threw down the firewood and sailed the pot and drinking gourd high into the heavens. They both landed with a loud CRASHHH!

Anancy, startled by the loud noise jumped out of his sleep only to see Osebo standing over him. He leapt to his feet and bolted off into the bushes with Osebo chasing closely behind him. Osebo ran and ran chasing Anancy until they both came upon a crowd of men carrying large guns, prodding and poking people shackled at the neck.

"Oh no a scary monster is going to get the leopard!" Ma'at's eyes widen. She leaps forward, sits poised in the middle of the bed and tugs at my blouse. "Will they catch him Mummy, will they?" she asks donning a half-frightened half-questioning look on her face.

"Well, honey bunny, you'll have to keep listening to find out what happens next."

"Okay, Mummy." She lies on her side tightly clutching my arm. I continue.

Since Anancy was but a wee bitty spider, he managed to crawl into a medicine bag tied around the neck of one of the women held captive. Upon noticing the men, Osebo stopped in his tracks. He had heard the stories from the other animals of the men who carried guns and took people into a wretched life of slavery. He knew better than to continue chasing Anancy. He did not want to be caught or worst shot by these dreaded men.

"I'll catch up with you another time Anancy." Osebo mumbled to himself as he retreated into the bushes.

Anancy grinned and marveled at how fast he was able to move and how easy it was for him to escape Osebo.

"I'm way too tired after all that running to go back home at this hour. I think I'll just lay here and allow all that tasty warthog meat to digest."

Anancy then falls asleep and is unwittingly transported onto a slave ship bound for the Americas.

The next day, he awoke to find himself at the bottom of a ship stacked up against hundreds of humans. Some cried, others sang, but most uttered strange words he could not understand.

During his perilous journey in the hold of the ship, Anancy had an encounter with Nyame, the Sky God.

"Oh, great Nyame," pleaded Anancy. "Please, please send me back home to my village in Asante. I do not want to be here among all these people wailing and crying, ailing and dying."

Anancy begged and begged, but Nyame refused.

"No Anancy, because of your selfish ways I have other plans for you. I am sending you somewhere, Anancy, but not to the land of Asante. You must go with these captives to the place called the New World."

"But, but Nyame," Anancy stuttered, "These people are slaves! I may have fooled Osebo and taken his meat but I did not have anything to do with them being here. They were the ones who brought me here. It is their misfortune to fall into the hands of the slave traders."

Anancy tried to bargain with Nyame for hours. But Nyame did not listen.

"Oh Nyame, punish the people who deal in slavery, but please send me back to my people."

"No!" repeated Nyame in a loud, stern voice. "I have watched you all this time outsmart all the animals in the forest and do things even great big animals were not able to do."

Nyame scratched his head and thought some more. "I have an important job for you in this new place. Here you can put your craftiness to good use to help people other than yourself for a change."

Anancy pleaded some more, but this time his fate was sealed. Anancy was not sent back to Asante. Instead, the Sky God sent him away to the New World. Weeks later, he arrived in Kingston Jamaica against his will where he became known as the comforter of the enslaved.

"The beginning..."

---

[1]The story, "How Anancy came to the America's" is adapted from its original version available at: http://Anancystories.com/Anancy_Came_to_America.html. Accessed May 31, 2011.

[2]In *Toni Morrison and Motherhood*, Andrea O'Reilly speaks to two key concepts that underlie the stories in this chapter: the motherline and cultural bearing. Citing Morrison and Lowinsky, she refers to the motherline as cultural maps or historical compasses from which female children refer to and draw on in order to know how to navigate the future. Also connected to this concept is the notion of cultural bearing: "the task of raising children in accordance with the values and beliefs of [African] culture"(2004a, p. 34). Both frameworks become central particulary for female children in terms of facilitating a literal and symbolic journey back to their roots. Through this journey, female children may uncover key survival tools and strategies used by their female ancestors that can help them

navigate issues such as racism, classism and sexism that their female ancestors also encountered. I consider this story of Anancy's crossing (as well as the personal narratives that follow it) as motherline stories to the extent that they allow the African child to tap into his/her African ancestral memory. I tell my daughter this Anancy story with the hope that it will help her locate herself firmly within this motherline of storytellers and storytelling so that later she will, in learning about the herstory of Africans crossing the Atlantic, develop a sense of self and connectedness to her African identity. This is especially important for me because, I grew up in a context where I was taught to loathe Africa and my African self. It was not until much later upon leaving Jamaica and becoming exposed to ideas of Pan-Africanism and Black consciousness espoused in the writings of Black freedom writers, that I began to consciously decolonize myself and nurture this part of my selfhood. My experience reinforces O'Reilly's argument that mothers, in this case African mothers, must have a strong sense of self and identify with their ancestral memory and ancient properties of the African motherline in order to be able to teach their children to be proud of their ancestry. This motherline story serves as a pedagogical tool for engendering in Ma'at a conscious knowing of her historical rootedness in Africa.

Webbed Toes and Fingers

SHE BOLTED UP THE PATHWAY towards their house. The glass shutter on the storm door swung back and slammed into her back. Cradling her books, she turned the keys inside the lock with the one free hand, pried open the door with her foot, squeezed through the opening, tossed her keys on the narrow glass table, leaned against the wall of the short hallway entrance, and darted toward the bathroom. She heaved into the toilet—violently.

"I made it just in time thank God."

She sat with her head slumped over the white ceramic bowl examining its content. Specks of yellowish pink and transparent liquid floated like miniature jellyfish swimming on the ocean bed. She grabbed hold of the rim, pulled herself up off the floor, wiped the sour drool from her face, flushed the toilet and turned the tap on. How—she wondered as she gazed into the bathroom mirror—could she feel so sick, so suddenly?

*

Trent University: April, 2005. Their meeting was one of happenstance. The sun shone brilliantly in the bright blue sky. That spring, they kissed on the park benches under the big tree, shared stories about growing up, and listened for hours to the droning sounds of him drumming on his Akete drums. As music junkies, artists, and spiritualists, they were kindred souls.

"Why don't we move in together?" Chakka asked.

She ran her hands through his tousled, black mane before replying. "Aaah, isn't it a bit too soon? We've only been dating a few months now." Her voice cracked, she cleared her throat. "It just feels like things are happening so fast."

He sensed her uncertainty. "I know this sounds cliché but we are made for each other. I mean ... you're always saying that time waits for no man." He paused. "I love you Ngozi. Plus I feel like we've known each other all our lives. Shouldn't that be enough?"

His lips broke and parted into a teasing smile that stretched across his oval shaped face. He waited for her answer.

Five months later they moved in together.

Six weeks into the new semester she began to notice changes in her body. He suggested that they take a home pregnancy test just to be sure. They peered at the plus sign as it grew brighter and stared back at them through the transparent window. Their blissful world was shattered.

*

Dazed and confused she gazed into the bathroom mirror struggling to come to terms with what she now knew. "What am I going to do?" she thought.

Twenty minutes passed before she managed to peel herself away from her face in the mirror. She walked slowly into their bedroom, pulled the heavy black curtains closed, stumbled into bed and burrowed in between her comforter and pillows.

Clutching the pillow closest to her chest, she laid in the darkness, closed her eyes and drifted off into a dream like trance. Shadows danced up and down the walls. With outstretched hands, they leaned in toward her. In her frenzied mind, the shadows took the form of women in her family who had passed away.

"Where am I?"

She opened her eyes and realized she was unable to move. Still anesthetized, she caught a fleeting glimpse of a ball of fire looming in the dark. The flames grew bigger, taking the shape of an elderly woman. She recognized the figure but could not distinguish her soot-eaten face.

The old woman moved in closer, grabbed her hand, and whispered in a comforting voice. Ngozi gave herself over to the beckoning voice that whispered, "my child, do not be afraid".

The old woman muttered on in an unfamiliar language. Ngozi tried to discern what she was saying. She couldn't hear anything but the maddening scream of a baby wailing, "Mamma". Its piercing cry was like that of a wounded animal. As the old woman spoke, a speck of flame leapt from her tongue and caressed Ngozi's face like the warm summer sun. The thick smell of parched skin filled her lungs.

Smaller specks of fire floated into the air, merged and grew into a separate ball. The old woman's phlegmed voice wrinkled like paper as she whispered, "Look", and pointed in the direction of the smaller ball of flames.

Ngozi watched as the image inside the flame took the form of an infant. "His face looks like his," she thought. She noticed his black wooly hair, how his skin glistened like a shiny new copper penny and how his small beady eyes shone distinctly from his oval shaped face.

Suddenly, her eyes are drawn to his tiny webbed toes and fingers. She noticed that although he looked no more than six months old, he spoke to her with the voice and wisdom of a seventy-year-old woman. She stared into his eyes just as she did earlier when she gazed into the bathroom mirror. In that moment, she knew he was hers. She knew what she must do.

*

In the midwife's office weeks later, she already knew before she heard the words, "You're having a boy."

Standing before the bathroom mirror that night, she admired the smoothness of her body, hoping to feel the first flutter.

Nine-Night

I WAS EIGHT YEARS OLD when I learned that a spirit world existed. I knew about ghosts—people who were once alive, who never crossed into the spirit world for one reason or another—and was petrified of them. Theirs were the souls that I became familiar with through the many duppy stories that my cousins told by the kerosene lamp at night.

I grew up hearing stories about Obeah, about people who performed witchcraft or 'black magic' on those they coveted or hated, about women who mixed things into food to keep their husbands or a straying boyfriends faithful, and farmers who placed trinkets under fruit trees to ward off potential thieves who ambushed their crops at night. I was told to beware of evil spirits, and that the most effective way to guard against spirit possession was to wear my clothing inside out or adorn myself in red. I was also told to walk backwards when returning home after dark so that I could watch for spirits that would attempt to enter the house with me. I was also taught to look away from hearses leading funeral processions, and to spit on a stone and toss it behind me if I called a dead person's name anytime during the day. Though the efficacy of these ghost-repelling rituals remain a puzzle, I performed them dreading that if I didn't, I would summon a bad spirit that would keep me permanent company. Later, I came to learn that there were also good spirits. Spirits that had crossed over and were contented. Spirits that became our guardians—our ancestors who protected us from harm. Spirits that came offering wisdom and guidance. Spirits that spoke to us through our dreams.

I was on summer holiday visiting my mother in one of Kingston's inner cities. Daddy always seemed apprehensive about sending me off to Mummy's house for the holidays. Mummy lived in an area of Kingston called Payne Land. Payne Land was an area known for its gang rivalry, peppered small concrete slab roofed houses, zinc fences, and its working class dancehall culture. For a long time, I wondered why so many of the houses looked like photocopies of each other. I later found out that they were built as part of a government project to provide housing for low-income families, many of who worked in the foreign owned garment factories. The factories, appropriately called The Free Zone, employed people in the surrounding areas (mostly women) who were paid very little per day for piecemeal work. The women—who served as a ready pool of exploit labour—would sit in overcrowded work areas slumped over sewing machines, buried beneath mounds of pre-cut cloth awashed in sweat.

These women, unable to organize or form unions to demand better working conditions, performed their work with a faint hint of pride knowing that with the few dollars a day, came a level of security and financial independence to provide the basic necessities for their children. Though many were aware of the true value of their labour, for these women, this seemed better than no income at all.

Mummy's house was small but it was comfortable and clean. The floor always glistened with the shiny newness of a silver coin. I later discovered that the cheap bulk "Wipe and Shine" polish mixed with a powdered red oak was what gave it its opulent sheen. Every Friday, Mummy would send us to the shop to buy a gallon of this white liquid. I would watch in amazement as she mixed it with the red oak dye and diligently applied the red mixture to the concrete floors.

"Yu suppose to can mek a part inna yu scalp once dis floor clean,"[1] she would say, as she instructed my sister and I on how to properly apply the treatment to the floors.

Mummy's home was a place of discovery, a place of freeness, a place for which I yearned. In the daytime, Payne Land would come alive swelling with the vibrant energy of children playing, dancing in the streets to the latest dancehall reggae hits that blared from sound systems. Adults and children rocked, whined and gyrated to the beat of dancehall tunes. I absorbed the lyrics of Shabba Ranks' "Trailer load a girls" and Buju Banton's "Batty rider" with relish. By the end of summer or Christmas holidays, I would return to my father's home eager to showcase my newly found skills. I would teach my cousins the latest limbo, tatty and, my specialty, the dance named after one of Jamaica's national heroes Paul Bogle—the Bogle.

At Mummy's, there was always someone to play with. Even when one of my friends were not allowed to play, I was sure to find company in another child who lived just steps away. We would play hopscotch, water war, dandy shandy, hide and seek, bend dung stucky—the Jamaican version of tag—and run around with neighbourhood boys in the streets without the annoyance of cars driving by.

I could enter and exit my mother's house in the daytime with little restraint. Mummy never worried. She knew that my sister and I were at some neighbour's house just a few doors down, that we were safe, and that we would come home once it began to get dark or we were hungry.

My mother's house had a small kitchen sandwiched by two bedrooms that also served as living and dining rooms. My older sister and I shared a small bed in one room, my mother and her partner shared the other room. In bed at nights while everyone was asleep I would lie awake disquieted, as I listened to sounds of gun shots bellowing, penetrating the night's sky. I was astonished at how my sister managed to sleep through the sounds. At first I was afraid. But after a few visits, I became inured.

We did not only hear these sounds at nights. On occasions, they would reverberate through the high-rise buildings on the adjacent street. In the daytime—no longer shielded by the fortress of Mummy's concrete slab roofed house—I was more afraid.

One day in the middle of our of hopscotch game, a hail of bullets erupted from the housing projects across the street from where we lived. My mother came running out the house with frantic eyes searching the streets for us.

"Go inside quick." She screamed, grabbed both our hands, pushed us inside and bolted the door behind us.

Panic-stricken, she yelled, "Go dung pon unu belly, get flat!"[2]

"What's going on? Why are we inside?" I thought. I wanted to ask, but dared not question her at that time.

"Soun like dem deh bullet deh connek,"[3] I heard Franky say to my mother.

She nodded. I was amazed at how he was able to tell the difference between the bullets that hit the open air and the ones that penetrated a building or another person's body.

An hour later, when Mummy's friend came by to tell her the news, we learn that Franky was right. My mother's friend, Coolie Man, had just been killed. Mummy wept.

*

I observed my first death ritual at Coolie Man's wake. Although my Aunties frequently talked about attending so and so's "nine-night,"[4] as my luck would have it, the ceremonies mostly happened while school was still in session. Because of this, I was never allowed to go. Since this time I was on summer holidays, I went to the wake every night with my mother and sister.

The wake was called a nine-night because the ceremony literally lasted nine nights. Everybody who knew Coolie Man gathered at his family's home on Top Road. Each night, the adults would share condolences, women exchanged memories, chanted old burial hymns, told Anancy stories, while men played Dominos and drank overproof Jamaican rum until sunrise. The final night —the ninth night—was most important.

This was the night when the family of the deceased prepared lots of tasty food. The night when children were given a small cup of Red Label Wine—I was never allowed to drink alcohol on any other occasion—to beckon the spirit of the deceased. Under a big tent in the middle of the yard, sat a table with kettles of cocoa tea, two thermoses filled with coffee, and six large aluminum baking tins stacked with loaves of hard dough bread. In the centre of the baking tins sat two larger ones brimming with fried sprat fish smothered in pickled onions and red and yellow scotch bonnet pepper.

I salivated. The smell of the vinegar laced with pickled garnish seduced and pulled me in the direction of the food table.

Suddenly, I heard Mummy's voice call out to me reminding me that I am not allowed to touch the food until midnight when the spirit had passed through.

*

The next day, the undertaker brought Coolie Man's body to Top Road for the final viewing. I held my mother's hand. My sister followed closely behind. The small procession of people marched slowly from Bottom Road to Top Road gradually ascending on the already swelling crowd.

Everyone in the neighborhood came to pay their respect. Some gathered around the casket forming a circle, others formed a queue to view the body, and I stood in silence anxiously awaiting my turn.

When I am next, I hesitate, not sure I wanted to see, fearful that I would not be able to erase the image of his face from my memory. How would I sleep?

Peals of crying interrupted my thoughts. Fear edged my eyes. I shuttered at the thought of looking. A lump formed in my throat and I mustered up the courage to take a peak. I stood frozen.

Lying there still with his eyes closed, he looked as though he was sleeping. I wanted to touch him. I reached in and placed my index finger on his hand. He skin was taut and cold. I quickly pulled my hand back and placed it by my side.

Women sobbed, wailed, and moaned, disturbing the silence. I scanned the crowd. My eyes became drawn to a woman in a dark blue dress. She donned a black hat with a meshed veil covering her eyes that stretched across her nose. She fainted. A group of women carried her away.

A lady dressed in all white—one of Coolie Man's relatives—grabbed his son, only months old.

"Di spirit haffi ear di pickney cry or im wi come back and play wid im,"[5] she said before tossing the baby over the casket towards the other side. A lady clutching a black silk handkerchief reached over the casket and caught the child. She tosssed him back to the other side. The baby sailed in the air and landed in another woman's arms. He belted out a loud cry.

The woman sighed, caressed Coolie Man's forehead, leaned in

31

and kissed him before saying, "Aright Coolie Man, wi mourn yu, yu spirit can cross ova now."[6]

---

[1]Translation: "You should be able to make a part in your scalp once you are done cleaning this floor."

[2]Translation: "Go down on your bellies, get flat."

[3]Translation: "It sounds like those bullets connected."

[4]In the Jamaican vernacular the wake is called a "nine-night" as opposed to a ninth night.

[5]Translation: "The spirit must hear the child cry or he will come back and play with him."

[6]Translation: "Alright Coolie Man, we've mourned you, your spirit can cross over now."

Chapter 2.
It Takes a Village of Mammas

Anansesem (Storytelling Nights)
Jacqui Terry, © Images Copyright 2012 (used with permission) www.jacquiterry.com

Anancy and Him Story[1]

"OKAY HONEY, WHICH SONG DO you want us to sing tonight?"

"Ummm," Ma'at pauses and thinks before responding, "How about Manuel Road?"

I sing to her the call and response digging song[2] she has heard countless times before...

> *Go dung a Manuel Road gal and buoy fi go bruck rock stone*
> *Go dung a Manuel Road gal and buoy fi go bruck rock stone*
> *Bruck dem one-by-one*
> *Gal and bouy*
> *Bruck dem two-by-two*
> *Yu finga mash nuh cry*
> *Gal an bouy*
> *Memba a play wi deh play*[3]

Most nights she is captivated by the sweet refrain. Her squeaky voice fills the air punctuating mine, and words she has managed to memorize from the previous nights' recital sputter clumsily from her lips. Most nights, we sing over and over again, until she falls asleep. Not tonight. Tonight, after dancing, singing, playing and when all my efforts at lulling her to sleep fail, I resort to telling her an Anancy story. I know how much she delights in me telling them.

Once upon a time and a long long Once upon a time and a long long time
time Anancy was a pass one oman Anancy was passing a woman's yard

35

yard, an him see her gran-pickney out a de doorway a read one story book. Anancy go sidung side a de pickney and start look ina de book to. De pickney tun ovah one leaf, an Anancy see one big picture a Puss pose off in a de book.

Anancy gi out: "Bless me yeye-sight! Koo Bra Rat! Tun ovah leaf, pickney gal! For if Puss and Rat ina book, me mus een deh to!"

But all de tun de pickney tun, an all de look Anancy look, him nevah see himself.

Anancy get eena tempa an teck a oat seh him mus put himself inna story book.

All dat time Puss and Rat was good good frien an dem always play de debil inna people house wid tief. Anancy meck up him min fi put a spokes to dem weel. So one day, him pass by a playin grung and see Puss and Rat out deh a play game.

Wen de game dun Anancy walk home wid Puss and seh: "Tap, Bra Puss, is how yuh dah play so nice wid Rat an noh eat him yet? Yuh know seh Rat is nice meat?"

Hear Puss wid him craven self: "True, Bra Nancy?"

Anancy seh: "True, yes. Nex time onoo meet up yuh ketch him and tase him so see!"

Puss tank Anancy and lick him mouth go home.

Anancy meck fi Rat yard.

Hear him to Rat: "Bredda Rat, me

where he saw her grandchild seated at the doorway reading a story book. Anancy sat beside the child and started looking through the book as well. The child turned a page and Anancy saw a big picture of Puss posing.

"Bless my eyesight look at Brother Rat! Turn the leaf little girl, because if Puss and Rat are in this story book, I too must be in the book!" Anancy said to the little girl.

Anancy looked and looked as the child turned the pages but still did not see himself in the book

All this time, Puss and Rat were very good friends who always played and made mischief inside people's houses. Anancy made up his mind to put a rift between the two friends.

So, one day he passed by a playground and saw Puss and Rat playing together. When the game was over, Anancy walked home with Puss. On the walk home he turned to Puss and said, "Wait, Brer Puss, how is it that you and Rat play so well together and you haven't eaten him as yet? Didn't you know that Rat is tasty meat?"

Puss responded greedily, "Is that true, Brer Anancy?"

Anancy replied, "Yes it's true. The next time the two of you meet up, you catch him and taste him and you will see for yourself."

Puss thanked Anancy and licked his mouth all the way home. They parted ways and Anancy headed towards Rat's yard.

Anancy said to Rat, "Brer Rat, I have bad news for you. A while ago I was passing by Puss' house and I heard his mother telling him that whenever he sees you next he should catch you and eat you because you are very good meat."

So after that, Rat started to avoid Puss,

got bad news fi yuh. Likkle wile as mi dah pass Puss yard me hear Puss muma dah tell him seh dat anytime him meet up Rat again him fi ketch Rat an eat him for Rat a nice meat."

Rat start teck weh himself from Puss, an Puss start meck afta Rat, an de two a dem min so deh pon one anada dat dem nevah got time fi tief.

One day one ole oman seh to Anancy: "Bra Nancy, me hear seh dat is yuh meck Puss an Rat fall out, an me haffi tank yuh."

Hear Anancy: "Is me, yes, De two a dem pose off ina story book and me cyaan go in deh."

De ole oman seh: "Cho, Anancy, dat shouldn't worry yuh. Me wi put yuh eena story."

Anancy seh: "How comes?"

De ole oman seh: "Me an all de odder ole oman dem wat yuh help wid Puss and Rat gwine tell yuh story to we gran-pickney dem a night time, an demo won't fegat it."

Hear Anancy: "Every night me wi come memba yuh something bout meself fi talk."

So every night wen de ole oman dem a put dem gran-pickney to bed, Anancy come an show up himself pon de wall or de ceilin so dat de ole oman dem can memba fi talk bout him. Sometimes wen de ole oman dem sleepy, Anancy tie up dem face wid him rope and wake dem up, meck dem talk bout him. So dem tell dem pickney Anancy story, de pickney dem tell smaddy else, dat smaddy else tell and tell, so

and Puss started to chase after Rat. The two were so busy chasing and avoiding each other that they had no time to steal food from people's houses together.

One day an old woman said to Anancy, "Brer Anancy, I heard that you are the reason Puss and Rat had a falling out, and I have to thank you."

Anancy replied proudly, "Yes, it was I. After all, the two of them have been posing in story books and I wasn't in these stories."

The old woman replied, "Oh Anancy, you shouldn't be worried about that. I will put you in the story books."

"How will you do that?" Anancy asked the old woman.

"Well, I and the other women that you helped with Puss and Rat, will tell your story to all our grandchildren every night. This way they will never forget them."

"Alright", said Anancy, "Every night I am going to come and tell you something about myself to tell your children."

So from that day, every night as the old women put their children to sleep, Anancy appeared on the wall or the ceiling and reminded the old women to tell his stories. Sometimes when they forgot because they were tired and sleepy, Anancy would release his web, tie up the women's faces and awaken them so that they could tell his stories. And from that day, they would tell their children Anancy stories. The children would tell somebody else, that somebody would tell somebody else until everybody was telling Anancy stories. Anancy made it so.

till me an all deh tell Anancy story.
Is Anancy mek it.

The story ends and I turn to Ma'at and say, "Jack Mandora, mi nuh choose none. Mi did lef something fi yuh, but storm-warnin blow it weh."[4] Her eyes flicker like the flame of candle on its last leg of life. She blinks, smiles faintly before surrendering to the world of dreams. Finally!

---

[1]The stories in this chapter speak to the theme of othermothering and community othermothering. In African cultural traditions, mothering is organized as a collective activity where women share responsibility for children in both informal and formal arrangements. Wane (2000) tells us that mothering is not necessarily based on biological ties, and that children belong to the community. In addition, as Bernard and Bernard (1998) explains, African women are also charged with the responsibility of providing education, as well as social and political awareness to entire communities. Similarly, Edwards (2000) argues that both roles (that of community and othermother) emanates from a long African tradition grounded in African centred ideas of communalism.

Most, if not all of my co-participants were able to relate to this model of community mothering. When I asked them to tell me how they defined or conceived of the role of mother, many of the women articulated conceptions of motherhood that extended beyond the gendered, nuclear motherhood of Euro/American feminist cultural traditions. Consistent with this view, African maternal theorists contend that the dominant Western feminist account which reduces mothering to an individual, private, and gendered activity is a problematic framework for African women, because it privileges the patriarchal nuclear family structure as the core social institution (Oyewumi, 2003;Wane, 2000). For myself and co-participants, mothering is and continues to be a role that expresses itself as nurturance, public work, economic and political support within a larger community setting (O'Reilly, 2004). Since this was such a strong theme, I decided to re-create stories around our shared experiences of community/othermothering. In effect then, the stories in this chapter are based on our memories of experiencing and/or functioning in this capacity where the role itself provided key pedagogical moments. As I was writing these stories, I scanned my daughter's Anancy and Miss Lou story book and came across the Anancy tale presented here (Bennett, 1979). My interpretation supports the views held by maternal theorists who see community/othermothering as vital to the nurturance, sustenance and survival of African communities and as an alternative to the dominant patriarchal ideology

of natural-intensive mothering (O'Reilly, 2004). This Anancy story told here to my daughter also becomes significant within the context of motherhood studies because it reinforces the importance of African women as the bearers of culture who (specifically in the context of Jamaica) are invested literally by Anancy and symbolically by the community with the responsibility of maintaining the motherline. Importantly, our foremothers as Karol Harroway states "carry the voice of the mother—they are the progenitors, the assurance of the line ... as carriers of the voice [African] women carry wisdom—[and] mother wit. They teach children to survive and remember" (1987, p. 123 as cited in O'Reilly, 2004).
[2]Jekyll (1966) describes digging songs as those sung during various kinds of labor under plantation slavery. These songs, along with ring tunes have been passed down throughout the generations and are a core part of the Jamaican folk cultural tradition.
[3]Translation: Going down to Manuel Road girl and boy to break rock stones. Break them one-by-one. Girl and boy. Break them two-by-two. Girl and boy. If your finger is crushed do not cry. Girl and Boy. Remember we are just playing.
[4]Translation: "Jack Mandora, I do not choose any. I left something for you, but the storm blew it away."

Sweet Shop

"I CAN'T BELIEVE YOU DID THIS. Taking sweets from a store? I just can't believe it. I raised you better than to go out into the world and embarrass me. Mamma Mueni is my name. Do you know what that means child? My name goes by your name. They all know you're my child. What you do reflects on me. I would have given it to you had you just asked. But to take something that doesn't belong to you is wrong. You know this Mueni."

Ten minutes of Mrs. Muttimos' rambling passed while they awaited punishment. Celia twirled her blonde, curly hair, gazed at her feet and fidgeted with the tail end of her skirt. Mueni hung her head in shame. She wanted to do something—anything but stand and listen to the painful thrust of her mother's words of condemnation piercing her flesh.

"Turn out your pocket right this minute!"

They exchanged glances before emptying the contents of their pockets onto the glass-top kitchen table.

Mrs. Muttimos' lips folded in outrage laced with a hint of disgust at the sight of the sweet wrappers. There were blue ones, green ones, purple ones, even the red liquorice ones her mother declared taboo—like beautifully crafted rainbow beaded necklaces they laid strewn across the table. She stood silently for a moment with her eyes riveted to the mountainous stash of forbidden treats, pausing just long enough for Mueni to get a word in.

"But Mamma...."

Dredges of shame surged from Mrs. Muttimos' lips stupefying Mueni, "Look at this mess here. Greed. Pure greed. This is no way for a child of mine to behave."

Mueni stood dumbfounded trying to avoid eye contact with her mother. Stomachs churned, saliva knotted in their throats as their bodies groaned and crushed under the overwhelming weight of Mrs. Muttimos' unending rant.

Mrs. Muttimos' gaze fell on Celia. "That is no way for any child for that matter to behave. You shame me, you bring shame to your Mamma as well. Mueni, go and get me your Baba's belt!"

Mueni looked sideways at her mother. She knew better than to resist as doing so would only add to her mother's swelling fury. She scampered reluctantly towards her parent's bedroom. Moments later, she emerged through the kitchen door trembling, her hands held out with her father's belt dangling in between her thumb and index finger.

They cowered in fear. Their bodies jolted as Mrs. Muttimos' hands grabbed the belt folding its buckle into her fist. The leather tail end passed swiftly over their thin dark brown and pail pink skin. Long red welts formed on Celia's legs. They both sat trembling, shoulders slumped, sobbing bitterly at the kitchen table.

Tears welled up in Mrs. Muttimos' eyes as she plopped down in the chair next to them. Her heart slowed and sunk in her chest. She could not remember the last time she was this angry with Mueni.

*

The Jones—Cynthia, Celia and Bill—lived next door the Muttimos' in an odd-looking-baby-blue-painted detached house with a white picket fence and beautifully manicured lawn at number 9 Haisley Place. Despite being the smallest house on the block, it loomed over the uniformed rows of drab brown-bricked townhouses.

Mrs. Jones was very friendly and quick to talk. She was, unlike Mrs. Muttimos, a conservative Christian who did not smoke, drink, or curse. She prided herself in being a homemaker. Her very existence hinged on how useful she was as a wife. She spent much of her days while her husband was at work weeding her yard, tending her roses, sunflowers and daffodils, or cleaning. Her predilection for gossip kept her buzzing from one house to the next of any woman who would spare time to listen.

Mrs. Muttimos did not care much for gossiping. But since she was home most days and since Mrs. Jones was the only one in the neighbourhood who bothered to stop by and welcome them when they first moved in, she tolerated her and eventually took a liking to her. On the hottest of days, they would gather around the glass kitchen table while Mrs. Muttimos brewed her special Chai.

"Where did you buy that lovely dress Cynthia?"

"Oh at Sears, it was on sale. Half off."

"Wow that's a steal, it's lovely!"

"I can take you there later today. They have them in different colours. And it will give me a reason to pop buy and pick up a pair of sandals I have been eyeing. You know, the flats ones you sling on just for walks around the town."

"Oh yeah. You mean flip flops right?"

"Yeah, those ones."

They would chuckle and tease each other about whose retail addiction was worst and how they were going to find a cure for it. On occasions, Mrs. Jones would take her daughter Celia with her to the Muttimos'. Since Mueni was new to Canada, had not started school and did not know anyone else, her and Celia became best of friends.

The Muttimos' was an open house for the Jones'. Celia would play the entire day with Mueni until it was time to head home. The two families became so close that before long, Celia was spending the weekends with the Muttimos'.

It was the end of summer—almost four months after the Muttimos' moved to the neighbourhood—when Celia and Mueni went on their sweet shop rampage. Mrs. Jones came by for her usual visit, only this time the conversation would not be about their husbands, children, or household items on sale in the Canadian Tire flyer. This time they had serious business to discuss—the thing that was on the lips of all the folks in the neighborhood: "Did you hear that Mrs. Muttimos spanked the Jones' daughter?"

Mrs. Jones and Mrs. Muttimos sat across from each other in the kitchen staring in silence.

"Can I make you some Chai?" Mrs. Muttimos asked trying desperately to break the tension that lingered in the air. Before Mrs. Jones could answer, Mrs. Muttimos leapt from her chair, moved towards the kitchen cupboards, rummaged through the dish drainer, slammed cupboard doors shut and banged pots and pans. Moments later, she propped her head up holding her special teapot.

Mrs. Muttimos was a Chai connoisseur. She knew just the right amount of milk and water to add to yield the perfect flavour from the dried tea-leaves. Her hand moved with precision as she measured tea-leaves, placed them in the soon boiling milk and watched with transfixed eyes as the froth rose to the top of the uncovered tea-pot before quickly removing the blend from the heat just in time for the froth to fall instead of boiling over into the stove. Seconds later, she would place the pot back over the medium-high heat for a second rise and fall. She would repeat this a third time before adding a ground spice mixture of ginger, cinnamon, cardamon, cloves, black pepper, and nutmeg, followed by a careful pouring of the brew into white made in China tea-cups.

Eventually, her stirrings in the kitchen were drowned out by the awkward silence that hung like a wet cloth in the gloomy air.

"Sugar?"

Mrs. Jones nodded with indifference as she eyed the supple movements of Mrs. Muttimos' hand dolloping sugar into her tea-cup.

Except for the sound of stainless steel spoons scraping the bottom of tea-cups, the air between them was damp and heavy. The quiet made Mrs. Muttimos uneasy. She finally gathered up the nerve to intrude on the somber silence that filled the room.

"I don't suppose you came here today to drink so you might as well say what's on your mind."

"Well, Celia came home with welts on her legs last night. Was that really necessary? Couldn't you have called me over or spoken to me about the situation?"

"Look Cynthia, the girls went out with me to the store yesterday evening." She paused and gasped for air before saying, "The whole ordeal was just so embarrassing. It was enough to see that store-owner looking at me with his nose turned up, talking down to me as if I were deaf or something, as if I didn't understand what he was saying. Then he had the nerve to tell me flat out that I couldn't control my children." As she spoke, her face bore the scars of the previous day's humiliation.

"I get that. I do. But there are other ways to discipline a child.

Celia has never been punished like that you know. Her father and I were very upset when she came home and told us last night."

"Look here Cynthia," Mrs. Muttimos hesitated before saying, "I understand why you are upset and I am sorry. But where I come from its perfectly okay to discipline children in this way. When Celia is in my care, she is my responsibility. I treat her the same way I treat my own child."

Mrs. Jones now red with anger paused and inhaled before spluttering, "Well you are not back home anymore." She plopped her tea-cup into its saucer spilling some of its contents as she raised from her chair. The jolt from her quick thrust sent it flying a short distance behind. The iron legs screeched against the wooden floor.

Mrs. Muttimos' lips wrinkled in shock.

Mrs. Jones snatched her purse and folded it under her arms. Her voice erupted, "Next time, I would appreciate it if you would run it by me before taking it upon yourself to spank my child." She started hurriedly toward the front door, turned back to Mrs. Muttimos and said, "if there ever is a next time."

Mrs. Muttimos trudged over following shortly behind her. Standing by the door, she peered out through the opening at Mrs. Jones as she careened down the pathway, hopped across the dark green-carpeted lawn before disappearing inside her house.

Tears edged Mrs. Muttimos' eyes. Confusion and shame teemed inside her.[1]

---

[1] In *Unequal Childhoods: Class, Race and Family Life*, Annette Lareau examines how individuals in social institutions selectively validate certain parenting practices as legitimate while designating (culturally determined) approaches such as belting unacceptable even as "spanking children was universally practiced in other historical periods" (Lareau, 2003, p. 230). In keeping with this critique motherhood theorist like Walkerdine and Lucy (1989), Ruddick (1989) and O'Reilly (2004c) provide two useful conceptual frameworks (namely sensitive and natural-intensive mothering) that helps us unpack why this occurs. They tell us that sensitive mothering is the ideological viewpoint that emanates from a white middle class perspective that the child should always be front and centre of the mother's domestic life, that there is no power struggle, overt regulation

or insensitive sanctions that would shatter the child's illusion that the mother is the source of all the child's wishes (Walkerdine and Lucy, 1989, pp. 20-24). Similarly, O'Reilly drawing from Ruddick (1989) explains that within the ideology of natural-intensive mothering the defining belief is that good mothering entails selfless and unconditional love for one's child/ren. "The ideology of natural-intensive mothering," O'Reilly contends is "enacted in the patriarchal institution of motherhood [and] has become the official and only meaning of motherhood, marginalizing and rendering illegitimate alternative practices of mothering. In so doing, this normative discourse of mothering polices all women's mothering and results in the pathologizing of women who do not and can not practice intensive mothering"(O'Reilly, 2004c, pp. 6-7).

Through both frameworks, we are able to see how individuals also partake in maintaining the ideology of sensitive and natural-intensive mothering, ultimately designating African women as m(others). Small wonder my co-participant (depicted as the character Mrs. Muttimos) displayed feelings of anxiety and confusion after this confrontation. The "fictional" character Mrs. Muttimos, now policed by the "gaze of others" (Ruddick, 1989, p. 111), begins to question what was for her an acceptable practice. Now under the microscope of Mrs. Jones, Mrs. Muttimos loses confidence in [her] own values" (O'Reilly, 2004c, p. 6) and culturally determined mothering practices.

Therefore, Mrs. Muttimos' "failure to use reasoning and her adoption of a belt made her vulnerable, since she moved in a field that privileged reasoning. If she lived a century earlier [or in another geographical context], the use of a belt would not have been so problematic. [In this context], however, it carries a potentially catastrophic risk: ...she could be arrested for child abuse, and her [child] be put in foster care temporarily or permanently (Lareau, 2003, p. 229-230)." Mrs. Jones' expectation that Mrs. Muttimos use other methods such as reasoning (identified by Lareau as dominant cultural practices and standards of child rearing) to deal with the girls' infraction is indicative of her un/conscious obeisance to the idea that the parenting styles of certain groups of people are always and already out of sync with dominant cultural practices.

Washday

IT WAS JUST AFTER SUNRISE, about 6:30 am, and my stepmother was already up. "Sweetie, wake up!" She yelled as she hurriedly entered my room. "We av nuff tings fi do before di sun go dung."[1] She fussed and frowned as she peeled the white cotton curtains apart and opened the windows.

Bold streaks of sunlight forced through the curtains landing on my eyelids. I squeezed them shut. When that did not work, I covered my head with the blue covers next to me.

"Wake up mi seh."[2] Mummy shook, prodded and poked my flesh before dragging the cover from over my head. I shuffled not wanting to get out of bed. I clawed my way from under the floral sheets, and climbed noisily out of bed knocking over the large goose figurine on the chest of drawers.

I planted my feet on the cold tiles.

"Ouch."

I squirmed. The cold penetrated their bareness like icicles forcing them off the floor and up toward my chest. I sat curled up on the bed's edge with my chin resting on my drawn-up knees and furled arms cradling my body.

I studied Mummy's movements as she floated around the room hurriedly, peeled curtains one by one, and removed them from the silver hooks holding them firmly into place on the white curtain rods.

My stepmother kept herself busy when something troubled her. She paused, momentarily, and gazed at my father leaving through the front gate for work. Bringing herself back to the present, she managed to escaped her own musings but avoided eye contact with me when she said, "Mi already saat out di laundry in di bathroom. Wen yu done washing yu face and brushing yu teet, gada up yu panty dem and put dem ina di sun fi soak inna some soap wata, yu hear mi?"[3] She continued, "Likkle girls mus know how fi wash dem undawear."[4] The words fell from her lips and lingered like a heavy brick on my head.

"Yu getting bigga now and nobody fi see weh inna di seat a yu panty dem."[5]

"Yes Mummy," I nodded in embarrassment. I threw off the sheets, slowly placed my feet on the cold tiles and meandered down the hallway towards the bathroom door.

*

Today I would miss the smell of thin dirt mixed with water from making mud puddings. Julie, Clive—the son of my father's friend who lived across the street—and I always played together. I especially loved playing house with them, but my cousin Julie, being older than I, always got to be the Mamma. Each day, her and Clive would sneak behind the bathroom stall in the old house while I pretended-to-be-baby-sleeping-in-my-crib, to play dugu dugu[6]—at least that was what we called it since we did not have the words to describe what it was we knew grown ups did at night.

Our house playing was restricted to the old house outside the view of adults. As children, we knew it was forbidden. If caught, we would be severely punished. Even still, I became aware very early that that kind of play gave me a sense of pleasure that in my child's mind was incomprehensible. On occasions, I would hear Julie giggle excitedly behind the bathroom stall as Clive placed sweet kisses on her lips.

Sometimes I managed to sneak a peak as Clive fiddled with the small tufts of hair on Julie's privates. I delighted in watching Clive's hands moving lasciviously up Julie's skirt as he explored the dark narrow spaces of her body. In my fantasies, I wanted him to kiss me—kiss me the way he kissed Julie. I'd watch as excitement collected inside me, and a pleasurable tingle surged through my body accompanied by a warm wetness. I thought to myself, "If this was what it was like being a grown up woman, I couldn't wait to be grown up."

Yesterday when Clive and Julie resurfaced from behind the bathroom stall, I fell out of my pretend play and confronted them.

"How come yu always get fi play di Mamma and mi always a play di baby?"[7]

"Well dats because mi olda dan yu,"[8] Julie responded in a voice filled with authority. I let out a loud "stewwpss"[9] before replying, "Who care anyway 'bout who older? Wi jus pretending. Tomorrow mi waan fi be di Mamma, or mi a go tell Aunty and Mummy pon unu."[10]

With surprised eyebrows and nostrils flared, they reluctantly agreed. I walk away thrilled, forgetting that tomorrow would be Friday.

Friday is washday—an important ritual for Mummy and her friends. Soon my stepmother's friends will gather in our yard, huddled over large plastic wash basins under the Ackee tree. It is the day for laughing, catching up on the week's gossip and swapping stories. It is the day when the women fuss about all the things that annoyed them; the day when socks and panties get soaked in the high afternoon sun, shirts get starched and ironed and I am ushered into the cult of womanhood.

Daddy sent me to bed early last night. I sensed that something was wrong. Did they have another argument about the woman who harangued my stepmother each time she saw her on the street? Either I was too sound asleep or my Stepmother did not erupt into her usual yelling. The only clue was Mummy's distance that morning.

At noon the sun was dreadfully hot. I stooped down over a tiny pink washbasin Mummy bought at Coronation Market for washing what she called my unmentionables.

The heat blared down on the back of my neck and shoulders. The Ackee tree casted a shade that did not protect me from the sun's unforgiving heat. I dipped my hands into the soapy water, fished out a bright green panty and squished it between my hands. They do not make that distinctive squishing sound that comes from my mother's grown up hand washing. White lather from the "Blue bomma" soap swallowed my hands as I massaged the white paste into the seat of my panty. Its acrid fragrance irritated my nose.

I sneezed.

Pixley barked alerting us of an intruder's presence. The latch on the front gate gave out a shrill squeak, screeching as it swung open.

"Weh Rose deh?"[11] A woman called out in a thin angry voice.

"Do, mi a beg yuh come and get mi before yu mongrel dawg bite up mi foot dem."[12]

It was Judith—she was always the first to arrive.

"Go weh yu damn dawg."[13] Mummy yelled scooting Pixley. She picked up a stone and threw it when he refused to move. The stone connected, hitting Pixley on the back-side. He whimpered, howled, and scurried off to hide under my father's old car parked in the middle of the front yard.

"Something is definitely wrong with Mummy today," I thought to myself. "She loves that dog. I've never seen her do that before."

"Him si mi every week an every week him bark at me. One a dees fine days dat daag gwine bite mi yu know,"[14] Judith said worryingly.

"Nuh worry yu self, jus gwaan roun a back,"[15] Mummy tried to reassure her that Pixley wouldn't bite.

Moments later, they both cornered the house. Judith leapt over the steps holding the tail end of her long airy yellow skirt as it ballooned out between her legs.

I gave her the customary greeting, "Good afternoon Aunty Judith."

"Good afternoon likkle miss. Nice girl washing yu panties. Yu Mummy teaching yu well."[16] She smiled approvingly, walked over to the wash area and plopped down on a bench next to Mummy and the wash loads.

"Mi seh Judith, one piece a sinting in ya last night."[17] Mummy continued washing as she told Judith about the argument between her and my father the night before.

The washday rituals were less about washing and more about catharsis. One of the women told the others her story, each woman offered an opinion, expressed contempt, or their interpretation of the details relayed. At times someone cried, other times someone cursed and exploded in a fit of fury. But mostly they would dissolve in laugher over some juicy gossip. They did this for hours until all the wash loads had dissapeared. After, they would return to their daily routine.

It was all so confusing to me. I did not understand the point of these sessions especially in my stepmother's case, since I, unlike the other women, was privy to the goings-on in our house. Each time Mummy would go through this purging and nothing changed. The next day, she would labour over a hot stove making dinner, Daddy would come home late, they would argue and she would let it all out on wash day.

Frustrated and scared all the same time, I rose up from my basin, walked over to where Mummy stood, tugged at the end of her skirt, gasped for air before hearing the unthinkable words, "Why stay Mummy, why?" spill from my lips.

There were many improprieties I could commit as a child. This one ranked high on the list. I learned by watching my cousins being scolded or spanked for breaking the code that children were to be seen and not heard especially when adults were discussing 'big people tings.'

My breathing became heavy and my heart pounded. I stood frozen anticipating a spanking, but instead Mummy replied, "Pig ax him mumma say, wha mek him mout' long suh; him say, ah no mine me pickney, dat something dat mek fi mi long so, wi mek yuh long so too."[18]

Still stunned by my brazenness Mummy's voice raised as she belted out, "Now go back an tend to yu washing before I lik you weh di sun don't shine."[19,20]

Relieved, I walked back to my place.

Stooped over my washbasin, I noticed a parade of black biting ants carrying specks of white bread crumbs back to a hole burrowed under the Ackee tree. I thought back to my stepmother's sullen face, her eyes welled-up, and her incomprehensible words. I sat twirling soapsuds around my fingers—watching the ants march to their nest—trying, but failing, to make sense of it all.

---

[1]Translation: "We have alot to do before the sun goes down."
[2]Translation: "I said, wake up."
[3]Translation: "I already sorted the laundry in the bathroom. When you are fin-

ished washing your face and brushing your teeth, gather your panties and put them in the sun to soak in some soap water, do you hear me?"

[4]Translation: "Little girls must know how to wash their underwear."

[5]Translation: "You are getting older now and no one should see what is in the seat of your panties."

[6]The word 'dugu dugu,' meaning sex/sexual play, is derived from West African languages of the formerly enslaved peoples (Reynolds, 2006). Even though we explored each others bodies as children, there was never any actual penetration. Because we were socialized to be chaste, little girls carried the added burden of ensuring that the boys did not go too far. Though this play was taboo to adults, it was very much a part of our informal learning about sexuality as Jamaican children. Generally speaking, adults were aware that this occurred. However, such explorations of sexuality were discouraged and suppressed.

[7]Translation: "How come you always get to play the Mamma and I am always playing the baby?"

[8]Translation: "Well that's because I am older than you are."

[9]A sucking of the tongue between the teeth that produces a saliva filled hissing sound signifying contempt or reproach.

[10]Translation: "That's not fair. And who cares anyway about who is older? We are just pretending. Tomorrow, I want to be the Mamma or I am going to tell Aunty and Mummy on the both of you."

[11]Translation: "Where's Rose?"

[12]Translation: "Please come and get me before your mongrel dog bites my feet."

[13]Translation: "Go away you damn dog."

[14]Translation: "He sees me every week and every week he barks at me. One of these fine days that dog is going to bite me you know.

[15]Translation: "Don't worry yourself. Just go on around the back."

[16]Translation: "Good afternoon, little Miss. Nice girl washing your panties. Your Mummy is teaching you well."

[17]Translation: "I am telling you Judith, there was one big fuss in here last night."

[18]Translation: "The pig says to its mother, "Why is your snout so long?" She says, "Ah, never mind my child, the same thing that makes my snout long, will eventually make yours long too."

[19]Translation: "Now go back and attend to your washing before I hit you where the sun doesn't shine."

[20]This Jamaican saying has been interpreted in many ways. Anderson and Cundall (1910/1927) provide an aesthetic and literal interpretation which reads: "The young are apt to be astonished at the deformities of the old but later on they experience it themselves (p. 68)". The saying was also used as a pedagogical tool to hone in on the importance of experiential knowledge within Afro-indigenous cultures. Now, years later, as I reflect on this moment, I realize that my Stepmother

was trying to tell me that I would experience some of the joys and struggles that her and other women experienced in their relationships.

Chapter 3.
Bright Eyes, Brown Skin, Nappy Hair:
Epistemologies of Beauty

Bath Time:The Negation of Self
Jacqui Terry © Images Copyright 2012 (used with permission) www.jacquiterry.com.

Nuttin Weh Too Back Nuh Good[1]

THE PLAYGROUND GATE SWINGS OPEN. Ma'at runs toward me. Radiating excitement, she soars into my arms and screams.

"Maaamee, Maaamee."

Her tall slender body weighs heavily on my chest. I am winded. She tightens her grip, muzzles my neck with her tiny hands, and plants wet kisses all over my face.

The daycare teacher appears in the gateway donning a look of concern.

"Maman, I have not good news for you today?" She says slowly trying to find her words. English is not her first language, and her French accent makes it difficult for me to understand what she says. I stand panic struck at the entrance of the playground. Her hands beckon, pulling my eyes towards my daughter's hair.

"Today, Ma'at cut her hair with scissors," her voice lowers as she continues.

My eyes fall curiously on Ma'at's head. In a frenzy, I scour my daughter's head searching for the evidence of her infraction. My breath quickens. I tug and pull at strands of hair frantically, hoping to find the tiny matted locks where I left them this morning. My worst fear is confirmed. I notice they are no longer there.

"How did this happen? Wasn't anyone watching her? It could have been worse. It could have been her eyes."

My anger grows more and more intense and I suddenly explode in fury. The daycare teacher tries to calm me down. She reminds me how quickly a three-year-old moves and that accidents happen in seconds. I stand and listen, tears form in my eyes as she recounts the moments leading up to the event.

"Mummy look I'm a Princess see," Ma'at says as she pats her hair trying to get my attention.

Still bilious I look down with transfixed eyes on the trimmed spot in the front of her head.

"Honey, Mummy is not happy with you right now."

That evening we walk home in silence. The stroller lurches down the road. I negotiate the cracks in pavement. The wheels trundle steadily, grinding and clacking against the sidewalk penetrating the silence.

*

The smell of peppermint shampoo fills the air in the bathroom and soothes me. My anger is slowly replaced with sadness. As I lather shampoo into my daughter's scalp, my thoughts retreat and I am returned to my childhood.

*

I am seated on a metal bench in the middle of the schoolyard. We play, we dance, we sing the call and response tune…

> *Round and round the ring.*
> *Yes Balinda.*
> *Choose di bouy yu love.*
> *Yes Balinda.*
> *A big head bouy yuh love.*
> *Yes Balinda.*
> *A dry head bouy yuh love?*[2]

Laughter rings out. I know next time not to choose the boy with tight dark rolls sprinkled like black pepper grains about his head. It didn't matter that I really like him.

"Nutting weh too black neva good."[3] I remember hearing folks say about women who were seen as unworthy. Undesirable. Untouchable.

I sit at the edge of the bathtub and gaze at the white ceramic tiles on the walls. For a few moments I am no longer there in the same room with my daughter.

*

I am seated on the floor in the living room nestled against my cousin's shoulder. The light from the kerosene oil lamp flickers across the concrete walls and six pairs of eyes beam out through the dimly lit room. The wind whistles and howls. The mesh gate on the empty chicken coop swings opens and slams shut. We jump startled. My Aunty Suzie must have left it unlatched.

From where I am, I peek out through the window at the stars shining brilliantly in the sky. Their glow splashes over my cousin's face who is seated encircled by us on an old straw mat. He lets out ghostly sounds that are invariably followed by the words, "*Once upon a time....*"

"...dere was a gal livin in Jamaica an plenty of man did want fi married to har, but she nevah want no black nor noh dark nor noh brown man; she did a look fi yella skin man. Well, Bra Yella Snake hear bout har, an meck up him mine fi try him luck wid har. Soh one day him dress up himself an goh courtin har. As him kin did yella, she teck awn to him and before yuh could seh "keps" dems married...."

Once upon a time, there was a girl living in Jamaica and a lot of men wanted to marry her, she did not want a black man, nor a dark or brown man; she was looking for a yellow skin man. Well, Brer Yellow Snake heard about her and made up his mind to try his luck with her. So, one day he dressed up and went courting. Because his skin was yellow, the girl took to liking him and before anyone knew it, they were married.

"Once upon a time dere was a black lady an she had a pretty wite daughta. De lady was a widda, and her husban—wen him was livin—did name Jack, an him wife use to call him Jack-man.

So nung de way how de gal was pretty and wite, all gole teet ina him mout... Well, the King hear bout dis pretty gal, an seh him hooda like fi get har fi married to...."

Once upon a time there was a Black lady and she had a pretty white daughter. The lady was a widow, and her husband—when he was living—his name was Jack. His wife use to call him Jack-man. Their daughter was so pretty and white, even her mouth was lined with gold teeth...Well, the king heard about this pretty girl and said he would like to marry her....

As little boys and girls, we learned quickly to grab hold of that which was outside our African selves—that the only way to survive in this world was to renounce any traces of Blackness—to straighten, to lighten, to erase, to amputate—to cut off the ugliness, to make room for whiteness—the thing others saw as beautiful. It was in that moment, sitting there slumped over the bathtub where I came to realize that the self-loathing epithets I had internalized but managed to tuck away in my consciousness still marred my childhood memories. I go over and over them in my head.

Ma'at's singing of the ABC song interrupts my thoughts. Immersed in play, she splashes about and tosses water from her "Mega Blocks" toy over the side of the tub.

Seated on the edge of the bathtub, I caress her head. I am finally able to talk to her about what happened at daycare today.

"Why did you cut your hair Ma'at?"

"Because, I want to be a Princess?"[4] she replies.

"Really?" I pause for a moment to think before asking, "So what does a Princess look like honey?"

"She looks pretty and, and...," she stutters before continuing. "And she has long hair and she wears pink like a ballerina in dresses."

My heart sinks hopelessly. I awash in a sea of fear realizing that my daughter has formulated ideas of what a "beautiful girl" looks like. I know it is not the image I have presented to her—not what I hoped she would gravitate towards. Slumped over the tub, I stroke the short dark patch where four tiny matted strands once hovered over her forehead. A whirl-wind of thoughts swirl through my mind.

What do I do? How do I make this right? Could she have cut her locks because she thinks it is not beautiful?

I carefully wrap a yellow bath towel around her. I hold her tightly and kiss her cheeks softly. Her limber head rests on my shoulder as I walk down the hallway towards the bedroom.

I rummage through her drawer and pull out her favourite strawberry printed pajamas, dress and tuck her under the duvet cover. As we cuddle in bed, the feminist mother in me wants to tell her that she is a person—not a princess—first; that she is beautiful on the inside and out and that she can be or do anything she wants to. I hesitate. "It's too soon," I think. I worry that she may not understand what it is I am saying to her.

I lie on my bed and peer out into the hallway at the hardwood floors. An ethereal glow escapes through a crack in the bathroom door. It spills out into the well of darkness and glides across the floors. I notice that water from Ma'at's bathtub brawl has now settled onto the floors in the middle of the hallway.

"I'll have to clean that mess up before I go to sleep." I sigh.

---

[1]In a 1990 interview speaking to Bill Moyers, writer Toni Morrison explains these experiences through her conceptualization of what she calls the "Master Narrative." When Moyers describes Pecola Breedlove (the main character in the *The Bluest Eye*) as one of the most pathetic characters he has met in modern literature, Morrison offers up the following explanation: "She surrendered completely to the so-called "Master Narrative," the whole notion of what is ugliness, what is worthlessness. She got it from her family, she got it from school, she got it from the movies; she got it from everywhere. The Master Narrative [is white male life] … is whatever ideological script that is being imposed by the people in authority on everybody else: That Master fiction … history. It has a certain point of view. So when these little girls see that the most prized gift they can get at Christmas is this little white doll, that's the Master Narrative speaking: this is beautiful, this is lovely, and you're not it, so what are you going to do about it? So if you surrender to that, as Pecola did (the little girl, that "I" of the story, is a bridge: [she] is … so completely needful … .she becomes the perfect victim."

Similarly, most of the women shared stories about their own struggles of internalized racism. Their childhood memories were stained by yearnings for lighter skin and all the other physical characteristics they quickly learned garnered respectability and general acceptance. In the context of our experiences, Morrison's statement is significant because the character Pecola serves as a metaphor for the many little African girls that have and continue to be bombarded by this Master Narrative. In reviewing the transcripts, what I found interesting was that these experiences (though manifesting differently across our various stories) remained a constant. This was so even for those who grew up in parts of Africa and its Diaspora where majority dark skinned Africans lived. The parallels in our stories of internalized racism are significant to the extent that they reinforce the existence of a larger story about the unmoving nature of ideological whiteness. The narrative of the "superiority" of whiteness is so pervasive that it shows up even in our knowledge production through the Jamaican Anancy stories. My storied representations in this chapter are my interpretations of segments of our shared memories as we dialogued about and reflected on how this Master Narrative shaped our awareness of self.

[2]Translation: Around and around the ring. Yes Belinda. Choose the boy you love. Yes Belinda. Do you like boys with big heads? Yes Belinda. Do you like boys with dry hair? Yes Belinda.

[3]Translation: Anything too black isn't good.

[4]I find the word Princess (when used to refer to little girls) highly problematic. Not only does it carry patriarchal connotations wherein girls learn to conceive of themselves through dominant standards of femininity and beauty, it is also a class-informed notion that reinforces sub-personhood relative to those conceived of as more noble.

The Erace(ing):
Trapped in a Pigmentory Prison

KIDS SHOUTED. LAUGHTER RANG OUT. Hands married, joined tightly forming a ring. Her eyes welled with tears. Her lips trembled. Rainey edged the circle of girls but there was no way out. The laughter roared louder.

Rainey sat in the dirt curled into a ball with her hands covering both ears.

"Touch her hair, Lucy," Sara urged.

Lucy smiled mischievously before reaching in and yanking the once neatly tied ponytail prominently displayed like a crown on Rainey's head. She ruffled her fingers through Rainey's hair.

"Ouch! It's like a scotch-brite." She paused for a moment, touched some more then continued chuckling, "More like a brillo pad."

Rainey cried, kicked and screamed, "Leave me alone!" at the others standing by. It was useless. There were too many of them. The circle of girls closed in tighter around her.

Another girl reached in and yelled, "Wow, isn't that something, it's so wild" eliciting peals of laughter as the others loomed menacingly over Rainey.

"How does she comb that thing?" Lucy asked puzzled.

"Forget about the hair. I wanna pinch her thighs, see if they'll turn pink."

"Yeah, let's pinch them. Let's pinch the black off Aunt Jemima," they taunted.

One by one they all reached in and tugged at her legs. Their fingers burrowed into her flesh like blunt table knives.

Tears mixed with mucus caressed the sides of Rainey's cheeks, dribbled down her nose and into her mouth. The girls chortled wildly and chanted variants of, "Booger face, booger face," over and over.

Rainey looked up at the vast expanse of blue sky. Feathering clouds hovered motionlessly. She squinted her eye against the sun briefly. She wished a black hole would open up and swallow her into the ground.

Rainey charged again and again and again into their hands until she grew tired and collapsed to the ground. Moments later, she got back up. She tugged, ducked and dove under their hands for what seemed like an eternity. Finally, she found respite in the unclasped hands of a girl who—in efforts to hold her stomach so that she wouldn't burst into stitches from laughter—left an opening in the circle.

She seized the opportunity to escape. She made one final charge through the opening, ran clumsily out the schoolyard, through the gate in the direction of her house.

*

That night, as she sat in the bathtub she relived the pain, the confusion, the struggle of feeling trapped in the dungeon of her skin. She reached for the bar of soap and dragged it over the bristles of the wash brush. She scrubbed and scrubbed and scrubbed; the darkness remained.

A knock at the door startled her.

"Rainey you've been in the bath tub awfully long. Are you okay?"

No response.

"Rainey can I come in?"

Silence.

The door creaked open. Her mother peeked in at her seated in the bath with her head hung low between her legs. Suddenly, her attention is shifted away from Rainey. Her eyes fell like an anchor into the rose pink bath water. Chilled by the sight of raw flesh with dotted specks of blood, she could do nothing but widen her arms and embrace her daughter.

Pain. Heartbreak. Disappointment welled up inside her chest. Rainey had been at it again. She tried—but failed—to erase the grief.

The sadness.
The source of her alienation.
The darkness.

Silky Straight

TWO BOTTLES OF "DIXIE PEACH" shampoo and conditioner sit perched on the side of the sink next to a small glass container of "Dax" hair grease. I eye the big teeth comb. It is mid-morning when Mummy summoned us to begin our bi-weekly hair ritual.

My sister would go first. Her hair is softer, easier to manage, and less tiring for Mummy. My sister's father was of mixed ancestry—Indian and African—so she was considered blessed to have had jet black, silky soft hair and loose curls. Even still, my mother decided to take all the work out by straightening it.

"Good hair" was what they said she had. I on the other hand, had tight African kink with rolls that lined the back of my hair line, stubbornly resisting my mothers' efforts to tease and tame them so they would lay flat like a new born baby's hair.

I would watch enviously as my sister came walking out the door with comb in hand, jumping down the stained red-oak steps, hair flowing in the wind. As she jumped, her hair bobbed up and down like a black silk handkerchief gently caressing her shoulder blades. Bent over by the waist at the cement casted sink, before water touched her head, her silky straight hair limbered.

Mummy applied the shampoo generously. She effortlessly lathered conditioner, passed her hand over the big teeth comb reserved for nappy hair like mine, and clutched the smaller fine teeth comb made for lighter, straighter hair. As she combed through the conditioner, my sister did not wince. She did not let out a sound.

I hated when Mummy washed and combed my hair. I welled

up with anxiety as I stood waiting, knowing that the experience would be more eventful, exhausting and painful for me. When my mother's attempts at coaxing me toward the sink failed, she dragged me howling, kicking and screaming. With my head now under the running tap, she struggled to keep me still.

The moments in between each round of shampooing brought temporary relief. Each time Mummy paused to dab more of the creamy yellow peach fragranced liquid into her palms, I managed to wiggle free—temporarily. I shivered as the cold water stabbed the nape of my neck and travelled down the back of my dress.

I screamed. Tears streamed down my face. I flinched whenever the big teeth comb scraped my already tender scalp and Mummy sectioned, softened and separated the knots with conditioner.

"Hold still unda di pipe nuh,"[1] I would hear her yammer on and on. "Mi nuh know why yuh fada nuh just cream yuh hair and mek it more manageable."[2]

Slumped over the sink, I cringed squeezing my eyes closed to dissipate the pain. Hours later, Mummy would let out a sigh and collapse in fatigue. My scalp would be red, sore and pulsating from Mummy's tugging, pulling and parting. I would emerge with hair sectioned into large plaits or Bantu knots—what Jamaicans called Chiny bumps—neck and scalp swimming in hair grease looking somewhat presentable.

I rose up from between my mother's legs, wiped my face, gathered the end of her skirt in my hands before asking, "Mummy, yuh can cream mi hair mek it straight like Terry own please?"[3]

I looked up at her with apprehension. Mummy's eyes emanated a puzzling sadness. I quickly lowered my eyes towards my feet. I waited, hoping for a favourable response.

*

Two weeks later, Mummy prepared my scalp with hair grease. I had been scratching and picking at it all week, forgetting that the chemicals once applied, would deliver sharp stings leaving behind a painful soreness that paled in comparison to the sharp big teeth comb.

"Beauty feels no pain," my mother would say as the biting twinge singed at my scalp. I didn't flinch. Not once. I sat and endured beauty's inexorable pain. It was a small price to pay to be free of my naps.

"Just right," I thought to myself as Mummy based my scalp, "Just right." Like my sister, I would finally have the soft, silky straight hair I had always wanted.

---

[1] Translation: "Hold still under the tap."

[2] Translation: "I don't know why your father doesn't just straighten your hair and make it more manageable."

[3] Translation: "Mummy, can you please perm my hair so that it can be as straight as Terry's?"

Chapter 4.
The M(other) in the Mirror

Anancy and Survival
Jacqui Terry © Images Copyright 2012 (used with permission) www.jacquiterry.com.

(Im)polite Violence[1]

THURSDAY IS FOR ME THE LONGEST DAY of the week. I wake up at 6:00 a.m., prepare breakfast, get Ma'at ready and off to daycare before returning home with just enough time to complete assignments for my creative writing class and skim readings for afternoon undergraduate tutorials. Moments later I am dressed and out the door.

Tonight is a night unlike any other Thursday night. I am exhausted and relieved the day is over. I wait in line at the front of the class facing the professor's desk. The ubiquitous emblem of the ivory tower—the blackboard—bears the chalking of today's writing lecture on "Parallelism." On the professor's desk sits stacks of papers, an olive green textbook, two smaller white course books, and a dark green file folder stuffed with our recently submitted writing exercises.

A woman leans over and scribbles on a piece of paper strewn across the desk. Students talk, pack away books, folders, laptops, and head towards the door. The desks and chairs once neatly arranged in a horseshoe fashion are now in disarray. I am next in line.

I check the time on my cell phone. It's 8:20 p.m. "Good," I think. "If I ask my question quickly, I should make it home in time to relieve Katie, the babysitter, at 8:30."

Suddenly, two white students—a man and a woman—approach and barge in on the queue where I stand awaiting my turn. I am swept up in a cloud of nothingness, taken by an all too familiar feeling of being present but not really existing.

I gasp. I feel air rush into my nostrils filling my lungs. I hold my stomach taut trying to think of ways to contain the liquid hot anger coursing through my veins emptying out into my cavernous organs.

I think to myself, "They must not have seen me. But how is that possible? I'm standing right in front of them. I know I am only 105 lbs., but my 5 feet 6 inches of height should make up for what I lack in body mass." I decide to say something even as I know and fear that any response to the blatant disrespect I am experiencing will only reify the pathology of untamed Black rage.[2]

"Hello?" I roll my eyes and wave trying to get their attention. "Am I invisible?" I ask loudly.

I catch the woman looking at me. For a quick second our eyes are entangled in each others'. She peels her gaze away and brings them back towards the professor.

The man ignores me and continues to speak. I stand thick with anger, I listen and wait some more. The rage continues to build up inside me. It rushes through me with such profusion, it was as though a kettle filled with water had reached its boiling point inside me and its content was desperately searching for an escape route.

"This is unbelievable!" I say screaming quietly on the inside. "Being the cool, civil, collected Black woman gets you nowhere. Maybe I'll go 'Tryone' on them, see how they like that."

"If I yell loud enough, or knock them the fuck out, maybe then they will feel the pain and humiliation I feel right now," I think to myself.

The man grins faintly and uses his body to block the space between the professor and myself.

"So, Dr. Jean" he says, "Do you think you would be interested in doing an independent study with me over the summer?"

The professor responds, "Sure. We can talk more about that at a later date."

Is he serious? That was what was so urgent that he needed to cut in line. I look at my cell phone. It is now 8:24 p.m. I will not make it home for 8:30.

Pleased with the response he receives, he gloats and saunters toward the door waiting for his friend.

An awkward pause ensues. I wait to see if the woman realizes what is happening and allows me to go next. She does not. She smiles a thin smile, asks her question, throwing her head back as she speaks. With each toss of her head her brown hair dances and sparkles under the halogen light suspended from the ceiling. Together, they walk out of the room with purposeful swiftness.

"Hey Adwoa, how are you?" Dr. Jean asks.

"I'm okay." I hesitate a bit. I want to say how I am really feeling but I am afraid the professor will receive me as the stereotypical "angry Black woman." Large tears brim my eyes. I hold them back.

"Crying is for weaklings. You'll never survive in this country if you do," I remember my mother telling me.

"You don't let them see how much they hurt you," I hear her say as I stand before the professor trying to find my words. "I had to fight, to scream to be heard, to be angry sometimes and so will you."

Suddenly, I hear the words "I'm so angry right now" roll like marbles off my tongue onto the professor's ear.

My voice cracks, "You are invisible even when you are a visible." The blank look in his eyes tells me he is not sure how to respond to what he is hearing. I try to tell him what just happened. He says he's sorry.

*

Carl and I walk home from class every Thursday. On the way home, I share the experience with him. He doesn't see the violence of racism. He doesn't understand.

"It's just plain rudeness," he says.

His words do not offer solace only more pain. I'm sure he thinks that I am making something out of nothing—that I've lost my mind.

"This is how it supposed to play out," I remind myself as he continues to speak.

It is one of those bone-chilling, cold, winter nights. The wind envelops my neck. I shudder, wrap my scarf tightly and pull the hood of my dark green parka jacket over my head. I look up and notice the stars are out. A tiny snowflake falls and lands in my eye. I squint. The warm embrace of my eyelid melts the icy particle. It dissolves.

I need some quiet right now. Carl talks on. I no longer hear much of what he says. I gaze down for a moment. My eyes are drawn to the swift movement of my feet pulling along the snow-carpeted sidewalk. Each step leaves my footprint etched in the snow.

At Bloor and Avenue Road I suggest we take the short cut behind a store. Moments later, we enter the lobby of our building.

Carl yammers. I hear him try to analyze what happened through the prism of rudeness. I roll my eyes furtively. My thoughts take me away from his droning. I reflect on the culture of whiteness[3] and the ways in which it manifests in sometimes insidious ways that render its violence unidentifiable. Maybe Carl is right. Maybe I am crazy to think two white students socialized into the culture of whiteness, who learnt to occupy space, to freely walk in and out of it without a care in the world for who was there before, who maybe never had the experience of that movement being restricted because of what you embody to act any differently.

Our conversation ends when I get off the elevator. I wave goodnight to Carl as his face fades sandwiched in between the elevator doors.

*

I peer out through my bedroom window and notice the falling snow has turned to rain. I pull the curtains closed, switch on the bedside lamp and crawl beneath the covers beside Ma'at.

I hear raindrops meteor down pelting the glass windows. I begin to tell her the story of "Anancy and the Cowitch Patch."

Once upon a time, one man did have one big pasture lan full a cow-itch and all him try him cyaan find nobady fi chop out di lan because everbody fraid a cowitch. So di man sen out one message seh any body weh can chop out this big lan full a cowitch him a go gi dem five golden cow. Well Anancy hear bout di golden cow dem and Anancy kin ketch a fya because him want di five golden cow. But just like everybody, Anancy fraid a cowitch.

Anancy go a di man yaad and seh:

Once upon a time, a man had a big pasture of land filled with cowitch. He tried and tried but he couldn't find anybody brave enough to clear the land because everybody in the neighbourhood was also afraid of the cowitch. So the man sent out a message with a reward. He said that anybody who managed to clear the land would win five golden cows. Anancy heard about the golden cows and he was very excited. He wanted the five golden cows but just like everybody else, he was afraid of cowitch.

Anancy went to the man's house and said to him: "Me, me Anancy I will do it, I can

"Me, me Anancy, me can chop out the cowitch because me nuh fraid a cowitch."

So di man seh: "Alright Anancy, mi a go gi yuh a chance."

But what him do, di man get one watch man fi go up inna one tall tall tree and watch Anancy. And him tell di man seh if Anancy scratch even one time, him naah go get the five golden cows.

So Anancy go and as him start to chop di cowitch start to fly. So the fus piece a cowitch fly and clap him so bups right pon him forehead. Anancy waan fi scratch but him nuh waan di watch man fi see him scratch so hear Anancy wid him smart self to di watch man: "Ammm, Mr. Watchman, di cow dem dat the man a go gi me, one a di cow dem have on spot ya suh?" And him rub him foreheard.

Di man seh: "No no, di cow nuh have no spot deh so."

"Alright."

Anancy gwaan and him start chop out again and anada piece a cowitch go so bups and catch him pon him knee. Him knee a scratch him but Anancy caan scrath mek di watch man see. So Anancy wuk him brain again.

So Anancy ask di watchman: "Ammm, di cow dem weh di Man a go gimme, di cow dem have one spot right ya suh pon dem knee?"

Di man seh: "No, no di cow dem no have no spat pot dem knee."

clear that land. I am not afraid of cowitch."

So the man said: "Alright Anancy, I am gong to give you a chance.

So the man hired a watch man and told him to watch Anancy from the top of a tall tree on the land. Then, he told Anancy that if he scratches just once, he will not win the five golden cows.

So Anancy went to clear the land. As he started to chop, pieces of the cowitch leaves started to fly all about him. One piece flew and landed right on his forehead. Anancy wanted to scratch his forehead so badly but he had to find a way to do it so that the watch man couldn't see him. So he called out to the watchman: "Ummm, Mr. Watchman, the cows that the man will give me, do any of them have a spot right here?" While asking, he reached to his forehead and rubbed the itchy spot.

The watchman said: "No no no, none of the cows have any spots there."

"Alright," Anancy said as he continued to clear the land again. As he chopped another piece of cowitch went flying into the air, landing right on the knee. His knee itched him so badly, but he couldn't scratch it because he was afraid the watch man would see and he would lose the five golden cows.So Anancy continued to clear the land. Each time he chopped pieces of the cowitch leaves landed on different parts of his body. And each time he itched he would say: "Umm, are you sure that none of the cows have even one little spot here on their backs?"

So Anancy gwaan chop again and di cowitch go suh pubs and catch him pon him back. And Anancy seh: "Amm, yuh sure seh di cow dem nuh have one likkle spot right here suh pon dem back

Di man seh: "No, no."

Anancy seh: "What about right yah so pon da side yah." Him scratch anada side a him back.

Di man seh: "No, no. Di cow dem nuh have no spot. Di cow dem clean, clean dem nuh have no spot. Den suppose one day dem walking and dem get one cut right yah so," and him scratch him head, or "right yah so," and him scratch him shoulda.

An a suh Anancy spen di whole day and chop and a scratch and a ask, "dem have something right yah so, dem have something right deh so." As him touch him bady him jus a scratch. Wen evening come, Anancy chop out di whole pasture land. An di man couldn't believe it cuz him seh everybody who come yah spend di whole day a scratch.

So, him seh to the watchman: "Yuh sure she Anancy neva scratch?"

Di watchman seh: "No, no massa: Anancy neva scratch at all."

An a suh Anancy chop out he whole pasture lan a cowitch and Anancy get the man five golden cow.

And the watchman would say: "No, no no."

Anancy would continue: "What about right here on their side?" And he would scratch his side. Then he asked: Then what if one day they went walking and they got a cut right here or right there." As he continued to point out possible areas on the cows, so he continued to scratch different parts of this body.

And so Anancy spent the entire day chopping and scratching and asking, "do they have a spot right here, or right there?" When evening came, Anancy cleared the whole pasture land. When the man returned, he couldn't believe his eyes. Up until this point, everyone else had tried and failed. Most spent the whole day scratching.

So he asked the watchman: "Are you sure Anancy didn't scratch?"

The watchman said: "No no Master: Anancy never scratched at all."

And that's how Anancy cleared the pasture land and won the man's five golden cows.

Lying in bed that night, lulling Ma'at to sleep, I struggle to erase the earlier events out of my head. "Am I invisible?" I hear myself say again, and again and again while patting my daughter's back. As I sing to her, my eyes fill with tears. They roll down my cheeks onto my pillow.

Ma'at turns onto her side. She sees I am crying. "Don't cry

Mummy," she says. "You want a smoothie?" she asks. I give her smoothies to cheer her up when she cries.

I manage to smile through the tears before saying, my voice soft, "No baby, Mummy will be okay. We'll both be okay." I feel like I lie to her. I reach over to the chest of drawers and flick the lamp switch off.

---

[1]Commenting on the symbolic significance of trickster figures in Afro-Carribbean folk tales, Daryl Dance notes that, "Anancy is generally a figure of admiration whose cunning and scheming nature reflects the indirection and subtleties necessary for survival and occasional victory of the Black man in a racist [and colonial] society (Dance, 1985, p. 12 cited in Pedrail, 2007). As in the story *Anancy and the Cowitch Patch*, the African mothers in this storied chapter serve as "resistant subjects" (Pedraill, 2007, p. 175 citing Donnel, 1999), that, like Anancy, utilize direct and indirect means to subvert (albeit temporarily) the dominant order. Other scholars have described this as an Anancy syndrome: a condition in which the marginalized enacts coded strategies of survival becomming skilled at trickery, deceit, manipulation and craftiness in order to survive the conditions of oppression. Anancyism therefore, is seen as a condition born out of the experience of marginalization which the oppressed uses to survive (Marshall, 2001 citing Barret, 1976).

[2]Johal (2005) in critiquing the white supremacist pathologization of the rage articulated by people of colour, tells us how Black rage has historically been used to describe the potential dynamite that is the black underclass (p. 270). Citing Harris (1997), who reconceptualizes rage through an anti-oppresive framework, he describes it as "the rage of the oppressed ... cultivated in an oppressive environment" (p. 273). Building on hooks' (1995) earlier arguments, Johal challenges us to move beyond this pathologized common sense understanding of black rage. Like hooks, he challenges us to recognize the positive, constructive and healing potentialities of Black rage as well as how rage can be used to activate agency, power and resistance on the part of the oppressed. Extending hooks' ideas, Johal further contends that Black rage, could become a pedagogical tool or a discursive/analytical framework for working towards social justice.

[3]Villaverde (2000) defines whiteness as "a systemic ideological apparatus that is used to normalize civility, instill rationality, erase emotion, erase difference, impose middle-class values and beliefs with an assumption of a heterosexual matrix" (p. 46). In its ideological manifestation and as it relates to peoples of African

descent, whiteness is a social system that promulgates the idea that Africans and bodies racialized as Black are insignificant objects and immoral beings lacking agency. This has been the basis and justification behind forms of (neo) colonial violence. The notion of whiteness functions systemically as a racist idea whose premise is that Europeans, our "intellectual superiors" are solely responsible for important and noteworthy economic, social, scientific and political developments within the human family.

Bending Gender

THE SOUND OF THE SCHOOL BUS pulling up to the curb brought Sophia out of her writing. She rose to her feet, moved hurriedly toward the kitchen window, and peered out at the snow-covered ground. She noticed a distant patch of grass once carefully planted near the pavement now struggling defiantly under the weight of ice and snow.

The yellow and black school bus stopped. The door flung open. Ziggy scurried down the steps of the bus and zipped up the asphalted driveway. The tattered storm door screeched open then banged shut.

"Ziggy!" she called out in a shrill voice. "How many times must I tell you to hold the storm door when you enter the house?" She paused for a moment looking at him before saying, "And why do you have to run up the pathway like that? You could slip and fall on some black ice and crack your skull open. Then who do you think is going to have to sit all day on a bench at Sick Kids hospital with you?"

"Sorry Mamma," he said chuckling faintly, his teeth glistening as a mischievous smile stretched across his chocolate brown-complected face. "And Mamma, don't worry, you won't have to go to the hospital with me," he added as he slowly removed his winter coat, pealed off his grey hat, black scarf, and brown wool mittens.

"You know, pretty soon we won't have anything left of that storm door."

From the doorway of the kitchen, the sun's phosphorescent glow bounced off her six feet frame casting a shadow that hovered about him where he stood undressing.

"The snow is going to come barreling in through that door right on top of us," she beamed broadly, looking out at him with devoted eyes.

He finished undressing and swiftly whirled down the hallway in the direction of the kitchen where she stood. Leaning in toward her, his still cold hands enveloped her with a chilled embrace. They shared a faint smile.

"How was school today?" she asked.

"Good," he responded flatly. He looked away, walked in the direction of the kitchen table, swung his backpack from his left shoulders, slung it over the arm of a chair before propping his bottom sideways over the same arm.

"Z," she said pleadingly, "Please don't weigh down the chair's arm like that."

"Sorry Mamma."

"How about I make you a snack?" Without waiting for him to answer, she scurried towards the refrigerator, pulled out a bright blue milk box, then reached into the cupboard for a saucepan, his favourite purple mug and a teacup. Her hands moved rhythmically as she poured the milk, added a spoon of cocoa powder, some honey and cinnamon sticks into the pan. She paced casually back and forth from the fridge, to the stove, to the kitchen table where he sat, then back again to the stove where she eyed the liquid slowly simmering in the pot.

She stopped suddenly, and in a firm voice she said, "Okay you know the drill, get out your homework."

He looked up at her and wrinkled his face. "Awww, Mamma, can I just watch a little TV first," he pleaded.

"No Z. Finish your snack then homework, then you can watch TV." She continued, "I'll look at the homework assignment while you eat."

The kitchen filled with the light of the afternoon's sun. Sophia leaned with her elbows pressed against the counter where she stood waiting for the milk to boil. Her eyes moved from the stainless steel pan on the stovetop, to the kitchen table, to the plate where moments before she had neatly layered and plated a tuna sandwich before him. She watched as he toyed with his sandwich, twirling bits of bread between his fingers, examining them from different angles pinching off edges of brown crust.

As he ate, he removed his books, a blue agenda and a yellow slip of paper from his backpack and placed them on the table.

"Finish that sandwich. You know we don't waste food," she said commandingly.

He leered at her then replied in a voice filled with annoyance, "Yes, Mamma."

"Boy fix your face," she said spooning out hummus onto the plate before him. She glanced over at the papers scattered on the table and caught a glimpse of a familiar sheet of paper beneath the small pile of books.

"What's that?" she asked, her hand pointing to the table where his books lay spread out.

"Permission slip for a school trip," he replied in an even tone.

"Another trip?" she asked incredulously drying her hands with a towel. She extended one arm across the table and picked up the yellow paper. She scrutinized the paper, twirling it around with her face scrunched up. She began scanning it. Her eyes moved swiftly down the page. She continued, "Didn't I just sign one of these the other day?"

"Yeah but this is a different trip Mamma. Mrs. Saunderson says this one is...."

"Yes, yes, I know. Mrs. Saunderson always says this one or that one is important. They all seem to be."

"It's a bus tour of the city of Toronto. We're going to the Native Canadian Centre and then we spend the whole day riding one of those double decker buses," he said moving about excitedly in his chair.

Sophia's eyes stopped abruptly at the bottom of the page. Her face grew tense.

"Fifty dollars this time!" she exclaimed. "These teachers are about to send me to the poorhouse with all these trips. Do they think I have a money tree in my house?" She raised her head as she finished reading, turned her glance toward him and said in a changed tone, "A tour of Toronto from an indigenous perspective. I suppose this is important after all. Even more so than all the other school trip notices they've been sending here." She placed the cup of hot chocolate on the table and settled down in the chair across from him.

"Thanks Mamma."

She nodded, "You're welcome, honey."

He quickly clasped his hands about the mug before raising it to his head. He gave out loud slurping sounds.

She beamed as she sat staring at him. She caught periodic glimpses of a look of delight on his face as he lifted and lowered his mug.

He was ten years old when he asked her, "Mamma, why do you..." he hesitated for a bit before finishing with, "...look like a boy?"

She paused, flustered for a moment, her dazed glance falling on her son. The stillness of the room left them frozen in time. They held each other's eyes for what felt like an eternity. His words weighed heavy on her. She lowered her eyes trying to hide the sharp stab of sadness she felt in that moment. She looked up again, reached out and moved her hand gently across his forehead. Her lips contracted tightly closing over her teeth before her mouth gaped open. She uttered calmly and softly, "We are all different Z. That's the beauty about being an individual."

He beamed his approval. The luminous sparkle of his dark brown eyes as he looked up at her filled her with hope.

She smiled a radiant smile.

*

Hours later as they sat on the carpet in the living room watching TV he asked her if she could paint his nails.

"Sure," she said. "Go get the nail polish from the bathroom cabinet. I'll do them up nicely for you."

She laid on her back with her arm stretched out at her side, her head propped up on a green cushion that had fallen from the couch. She looked off pleasingly as he danced across the living room, down the hallway eventually disappearing into the small bathroom. As she lay sprawled on the carpeted floor, she thought of the question he had asked. She waited for him to return.

Killing Me Softly

I SAT ON THE SAT ON THE FLOOR beside the oversized windows with my legs crossed scanning my trove of high school photographs. As I gazed out at the expanse of blue sky, the deceptive sunlight shining through the windows beckoned to me. I do not submit. Having lived here long enough I know better. Even as the sun's scattered beams caressed my face and warmed my shoulders, I know that it is freezing outside.

I thought back to the summer of 1998—the year I turned fifteen. It was the year I graduated from Wolmers' High School for Girls; the year my father received the news that my long awaited papers being filed by Mummy through Citizenship and Immigration Canada had been approved; the year I said goodbye to my Island home and boarded a plane for what was to become my new home, Toronto.

Seated on my apartment floor I saw my first day at my new high school. Mummy and I sat between two girls on a row of benches outside the guidance counselor's office. A man, in his late sixties perhaps, face blemished by age lines with thin hair stretched pasted across his balding forehead appeared in the hallway. His cherry pink, thin lips parted into a smile that inched wider and wider across his ghostly pale face. He scanned a piece of paper attached to a clipboard in his hand, looked out into the hallway through brilliant blue doe-eyes that glistened through his rounded spectacles before calling out in and unexpectedly harsh raspy voice, "Williamson you can come in now."

As he walked down the hallway in front of us, his uneven gait drew my attention. He hobbled on one foot dragging the other closely behind him. He led us into his office, closed the door, shook my mothers' hand, introduced himself (Mr. Albanese was his name) before sitting in a big armed, dark brown leather chair that swallowed his slender frame. Except for the mahogany stained desk intruding on the space between the guidance counselor and us, the office had very little furniture. Even still, the air inside the dimly lit room weighed heavy.

Off to one side of the desk in a corner stood a vintage coat hanger embossed with ornate vines and flowers meticulously crafted onto a wrought-iron rod. The vines danced around the pole eventually spilling out into an open claw at the top where a felt hat sat comfortably.

On the opposite side, stood a filing cabinet that also doubled as a shelf. On the shelf sat a lamp whose depressing glow flickered into the small space gradually dying as it landed onto the bare off-white walls. I gazed at the odd looking large yellow shade meticulously painted with pictures of horses running in an open field.

He opened his mouth to speak. His words poured with such profusion they surged through the yawning gap that was his mouth, spilled over his crooked yellow teeth before leaping and landing onto my mother and I. As he spoke, the flesh separating Mummy's freshly plucked eyebrows furled. They remained unyielding as he continued to speak. My mother, now overwhelmed by the volley of words—words she knew nothing about—offered up the only response she could, her still furrowed brow.

I sat quietly scribbling notes in my notepad. Leaning forward on the edge of my chair, I glanced at the pile of papers he stacked before Mummy.

She looked away surreptitiously.[1] Reaching down deep into her large patent leather handbag, I could here her greedy air brushed acrylic nails claw through loose change, compact, wallet and a pair of scissors—my mother always carried a pair of scissors in her purse—before making their way to an opening in the side of the purse. Her hand surfaced, clutching a zip lock bag filled with report cards from my old high school, transcripts, immunization cards and immigration papers. She placed the bag on the desk before him.

His eyes darted away from the package towards Mummy's face.

He continued to tell her what courses I should enroll in, quickly mulling over the difference between basic and advance level courses. Mr. Albanese's words rained on Mummy trickling down like water running off a duck's back.

"Mrs. Williamson," then pausing and clearing his throat before continuing, "Hmm, hmmm, it is Mrs. is it?" Mummy nodded, looked at him with disdain knowing that the question he really wanted to ask was, "Are you married?" He continued to speak. Mummy listened intently trying to digest his word. He continued, "I recommend that she take all the basic courses to start just so she could get used to the system."

He stopped talking. I managed to squeeze a few words in.

"I don't want to do basic level courses, I can do the advance ones."

He sat motionless staring at me. His pale face suddenly looked feverish. I leered back at him defiantly.

"You speak English very well," he said in an incredulous tone.

I wanted to respond with, "The British colonial lackeys in Jamaican schools spent years shoving English down my throat from the moment I started kindergarten. Of course I speak English!" I wanted to let out a scream of protest. A violent fury welled up inside me emboldening me to say in a still petulant voice, "Yes, of course I do. And I will do just fine taking the advance level courses." I heard my Jamaican accented English weave its way through my words quickly filling the small room.

I shrugged in contemptuous reproach lifting the ziplock bag from his desk before handing it back to Mummy. His recently spoken words rolled around like marbles in my head. I sat and stared off into the grim distance thinking: a man who assumed without knowing anything or caring to know anything about me, who thought I was intellectually inferior was deciding my future. That day, I left the office bereft of hope of surviving in that school. By the time I walked through the glass doors of his office, down the freshly polished corridors, the hurt, the sadness, the despondency slowly dissipated.

*

It was still light out when Mummy and I left the guidance counsellor's office that day. A faint glow from the brilliant reddish orange sunset pressed against the sky suspended itself behind the sprawling brown buildings that lined Jane Street and Lawrence Avenue West.

As we hurried down Lawrence Avenue West, I thought about finding something to eat. My stomach growled loudly. Mummy heard. We looked at each other and laughed out loudly.

Strolling pass the Money Mart at the corner of Weston Road and Lawrence Avenue, I saw a car parked off to the side of road with a man seated inside wearing an orange T-shirt. The car pulsated with a hip-hop beat as Lauryn Hill belted out, *"Killing me softly with his song, killing me softly with his song, telling my whole life with his words, killing me softly."* The car hurled bass into the streets provoking rapid movements from the hips of two girls standing by a bench at the bus stop.

We walked on passing a kaleidoscope of banks, fast food joints, a barbershop, and a store displaying an array of colourful hair weaves and "African beauty products" all closely pressed together until we eventually slowed at the entrance of a store where a sign suspended on metal rods read "Chu's Convenience and Variety Store." A smaller red and white "Come in, we're open" laminated sign on the glass door beckoned us. The door let out a shrill ding-dong as Mummy pushed it open. I followed.

The aroma of freshly baked bread bothered my nose. My mouth swelled with saliva as we strode towards the counter where a short small-eyed, frail, sixtyish-looking woman peeked over the cash register smiling. Mummy placed her order and slid a toonie and a loonie across the glass counter.

The woman extended her hands, punched a few keys on the cash register, deposited the change in the drawer before hobbling off, disappearing into the back of the store. Moments later, she surfaced holding two crispy hot-out-of-the-oven Jamaican beef patties sandwiched between two cocoa breads—just the way we would have it back home. The glass door chimed again as we pulled it open. We continued in the direction towards our apartment building.

---

[1]In this moment, my mother's silence may be interpreted as her surrendering or

conceding to the master narrative that is white supremacy. However, when viewed through a different lens within a racialized context, the Jamaican saying "you play fool fi ketch wise" (that is, you resort to Anancyism: pretend to be foolish to trip up those who are perceived to be, and who think of themselves as wiser and stronger) rings true. Prior to this, I had witnessed my mother having to deal with social services and other state agents. In those encounters my mother was very vocal in vehemently rejecting the dominant scriptings of her body and the over policing of her mothering practices. Hence, I was quite taken aback and disappointed by her silence here. Reflecting on this event years later, I have learnt that silent or non-verbal rage is also an expression of resistance (Boylorn, 2011). When interpreted through the prism of the Anancy trickster figure, I now see that her body posture, her furrowed eyebrow and her silence spoke very loudly as "camouflaged resistance" (Pedraill, 2007, p. 175). I now see this as one of her ways of coping with and navigating whiteness and its attendant scripting of her body as an unwed, "unintelligent" Black mother. Rather than verbalize her rage in this encounter with the guidance counsellor, my mother chose to use another tactic which she perhaps thought would help her preserve energy and mental health to fight other battles. Until recently, I had not imagine that there were other mechanisms that I could avail myself of in this fight that my mother once cautioned me I would have to engage in to survive in Canada.

Chapter 5.
I Feel Therefore I Can … (Be)long

The Wisdom of a Child
Jacqui Terry © Images Copyright 2012 (used with permission) www.jacquiterry.com.

Anancy and Common Sense[1]

"STORY TIME MA'AT!" I CALL OUT to her in the living room where she sits on a blanket trancedly watching *Dora the Explorer* on a once white comforter now stained by series of grape juice and chocolate almond milk spills. When she does not respond, I waltz into the living room and stoop down beside her. Pulling her toward me, I collect her coiled body into my arms.

She squirms about. Her unfurled legs fall free. They hit the floor, splatter like a boulder and sprawl out.

As I playfully tickle her sides and armpits, I pinch her nose and drag her towards the bed. She purses her lips shut. They eventually spill open into a quivering cackle. She tries to wiggle free as I manage to wrestle her to the bed. She tunnels her body under the covers then floats her head up in between an air pocket separating the duvet from its thin white cotton cover.

Reaching across the chest of drawers, I pick up her Anancy and Miss Lou storybook.

"Would you like to turn the pages as I read?"

She sighs softly. Then, resting her head on my arm, she nods and smiles a childlike smile.

"Okay," I say in a quite voice. "This story is called "Anancy and Common Sense.""

Once upon a time Anancy tink to himself seh dat if him coulda collect up all de common-sense ina de worl an keep it fi himself, den him bound fi

"Once upon a time Anancy got this idea that he could collect all the common sense in the world and keep it to himself. That way he could get a lot of money and power because, everybody would come to him

get plenty money and plenty powah, for everybody would haffi come to him wid dem worries an him woulda charge dem very dear wen him advise dem.

Anancy start fi collect up all de common-sense him could fine and put dem ina one big-big calabash. Wen him search and search and couldn't' fine no more common-sense, Anancy decide fi hide him calabash full a common-sense pon de top of a high-high tree which part nobody else coulda reach it.

So, Anancy tie a rope round de neck a de calabash and tie de two end a de rope togedda, an tie de rope roun him neck so dat de calabash wasa res pon him belly. Anancy start fi climb up de high-high tree, which part him was gwine hide de calabash, but him couldn't climb too good nor too fas, for de calabash wasa get in him way everytime him try fi climb. Anancy try and try so till all of a sudden him hear a bwoy a stan up a de tree root an a laugh an halla she: "What a foo-fool man! If yuh want to climb de tree front ways, why yuh don't put de calabash behine yuh?"

Well sah, Anancy soh bex fi hear dat big piece a common-sense come outa de mout a such a likkle bit a bwoy afta him did tink dat him did collect all de common-sense in the worl, dat Anancy grab off de calabash from roun him neck an fling it dung a de tree root, an de calabash

with their troubles and he would charge them a high price for advice.

So, Anancy started out to collect all the common sense he could find and put it in a big calabash. When he searched and searched and could not find any more common sense, Anancy decided to hide the calabash filled with common sense in the top of the tallest tree in the village where no one else could reach it.

Anancy then tied a rope around the neck of the calabash and attached the calabash to his stomach. After which, he attempted to climb the tree. In trying to climb, Anancy realized that he couldn't make it up the tree where he wanted to hide the calabash.

Each time he would jump onto the tree, he would fall down. Even still, Anancy kept on trying. After hours and numerous attempts he suddenly heard a little girl's voice calling out to him at the foot of the tree: 'Anancy you are so foolish. Don't you know that if you want to climb the tree, it's best to put the calabash on your back? That way you can move up the tree easier.'

Anancy looked down in shock at the little girl standing at the tree's stump. He was quite upset to hear that big piece of common sense come out of the mouth of such a little girl. He was certain that he had collected all the common sense and that there was no more left in the world. Enraged, Anancy yanked the calabash from around his neck and threw it to the ground. The calabash broke into pieces and all the common sense floated and scattered all over the world. And from that day onwards, everybody got a little bit of common sense."

bruck up in minces an de common-sense dem scatter out ina de breeze all ovah de worl an everybody get a lickle bit a common-sense.

I issue the customary: "Is Anancy mek it suh. Jack Mandora, me nuh choose none."[2]

I close the book and place it on my lap.

"Look Mummy!" Ma'at exclaims pointing towards the crack in the curtains. "It's dark outside. The sun is gone to sleep."

"Yes. And you know who else has gone to sleep? Angel, Emma and all your friends at daycare," I say leaning in to her with the tip of my index finger gently pressed against her tiny button nose.

"Do you know what that means? It means it's time for Ma'at to go to sleep too."

"But Mummy, I don't wanna go to sleep." She blinks and rubs her eyes even as she protests.

Fatigued and frustrated, I blurt out, "Ma'at it is 11 o'clock. It's much too late to do this. Not when I am tired. Please go to sleep!"

She protests some more. The timbre shift in my voice startles her when I continue saying, "THIS IS NOT NEGOTIABLE. NOT TONIGHT!"

Sedated, she looks up at me glossy-eyed, tears leaking from the side of her face.

Staring down at her, shockwaves of guilt run through my body. Even as I speak with my mouth, the voice I am hearing is that of my mothers' commanding her to do as I say.

"Ave some respek fi yuh eldas,"[3] my stepmother, or some aunt would say or, "Young bud nuh know storm,"[4,5] words reminding me to unquestioningly submit to their eldership. This was the part of being a child that I abhorred. The part of growing up without even a little bit of freedom to choose—or to at least talk about why it was that I did not want to do something, or eat something, or go somewhere but was still made to because an elder said—without ever explaining—that I just had to.

Suddenly, I begin to imagine myself as a three-year-old. What must that be like? I think to myself. How do I create a balance without contradicting the story I just read to her? Perhaps dictating what she ought to do is not the best approach given that there aren't too many instances—at least for a few more years—where she will be allowed to exercise some degree of agency. The questions float about in my head as I lay beside her listening to her muffled sobs.

I turn to her and ask, "Why don't you want to go to sleep Ma'at?"

She pauses crying then responds, her small wounded voice quivering, "Because I am not tired Mummy." A long silence follows. I do not know any other way to respond to her.

She looks up at me with a sullen face, yawns widely before saying, "Mummy, baby need you to rock her."

"Really. I thought this morning you told me you were not a baby?" I asked smiling.

Pats of my palm land in the centre of her back carrying with it spiny vibrating sounds whose hollowness hum through the quiet night. I tell her that she is getting to be a big girl and that big girls need their rest so that they can wake up with the sun and be strong enough to play all day.[6]

"Mummy, am I a big girl?" she asks now smiling.

"Sure you are. And soon you will get to do lots of fun things on your own. But now it's time to go to bed okay?"

"Okay, Mummy." She turns her head and says, "But there's something missing."

"What's missing?"

"A lullaby."

"Okay, which one do you want me to sing?"

Her small, sleep-choked voice selects the song she wants to hear. She yawns the first few words. Whispering, I continue singing the chorus of her favourite lullaby: "Laa, laa, toto lalaa Mamma ana kuja laa laa."[7]

I croon softly, my voice fades thinly into the night. Eyes now laden, Ma'at falls asleep.

---

[1]The stories in this chapter were developed in response to some of the issues and themes raised in the previous chapters. They mark the beginning of my exploration into the pedagogical relevance of "mothering peoples"(O'Reilly and Ruddick, 2009, p. 31) of African descent and in particular women identified African mothers. They illustrate how African women engage in and combine maternal

practice—described as the work that mothers engage in when they set out to fulfill the demands of mother-work (nurturing, protection, training and cultural bearing) and maternal thinking —described as the specific discipline of thought, a cluster of attitudes, beliefs and values that arise out of engaging in motherwork (O'Reilly, 2004; Ruddick, 1989) to produce maternal pedagogies—the art, science and/or act of teaching that one engages in through motherwork and that is un/consciously informed by a critical feminist consciousness, that challenges all forms of oppressions and is geared toward social justice and equity (Green, 2006, 2009a, 2011; Green & Bird, 2011).

The stories attest to the potentialities of a purposeful feminist maternal pedagogies informed by the embodied knowledges of African women. They show how the African mother's lived experiences and culturally specific African feminist practices can engender critical consciousness, self-naming/definition and a stronger sense of belonging. Therefore, African women who "mother" serve as a site from which the African child learns about their existential situation, becomes equipped to critically interrogate status quo ideas, and resist marginalizing tendencies of the master narrative. Maternal thought and practice that is informed by a race, gender, class consciousness; a consciousness of the workings of ableism, sexism, homophobia, patriarchy and white supremacy; a teaching that is shaped by a rootedness in African cultural traditions, in African ideas about the liberation of African peoples and the embracing of an African sense of self is an articulation of African maternal pedagogies.

[2]Translation: Anancy made it so. Jack Mandora, I don't choose any.

[3]Translation: Have some respect for your elders.

[4]Translation: A young bird does not know how to weather the storm.

[5]This essentially spoke to the relative inexperience of youth in terms of their lack of exposure to the sometimes harsh realities of life. The saying was often issued as a call to the younger generation to recognize the wisdom and knowledge that elders possessed. Therefore, the onus was on elders in our community to guide the younger generation in navigating life's storms.

[6]This encounter with my daughter provided an opportunity for me to interrogate the method of authoritarian parenting I was exposed to growing up. Now, being a mother, I take cues from and engage in what Sara Ruddick calls maternal thinking" defined more precisely as: "the cognitive capacity to welcome change and to change with change." She continues stating, "[those who change with change and welcome its challenges acquire a special kind of learning ... maternal experience with change and the kind of learning it provokes will help us to understand the changing natures of all peoples and communities (O'Reilly and Ruddick, 2009, p. 23)." My maternal thinking evidenced here is informed by a consciousness of power relations and their implications for reinforcing relations of domination. I realize that my relationship with my daughter is indeed a relationship of power.

However, I am also aware that it may not necessarily be so. As the holder of power in our relationship, I can choose to not exercise the power that I have so that she does not always feel like I am the sole authority whose rules she has to follow without question.

While I am not always able to negotiate this power in the moment, and often revert to the parenting practices I was exposed to as a child, I consciously try to create space to allow Ma'at to pose critical questions and challenge me. Similar to other feminist theorists and teachers, I start from the premise that my daughter is a person who has thoughts, feelings and ideas that matter. More importantly, I have come to value and validate her insights realizing that she also has knowledge to share. I am now able to see her questions as more than mere challenges to my authority but as resources and opportunities for learning as I engage in motherwork. It is in this regard that the story *Anancy and Common Sense* becomes a piece of feminist pedagogy. Embedded in the story, is the idea that even a small child embodies knowledge that an adult could gain from. Interpreted in this way, the teachings in this Anancy story empower her to ask challenging questions, to think critically and articulate her ideas even if it is not in keeping with the perspectives of others and my own. It provides an opportunity for her to learn that she "is [also] significant in a world where [her] realities are often denied and where adults overpower children"(Green, 2011, p. 203).

[7]Translation: "Sleep, baby, sleep. Mamma is coming, sleep."

In My Mamma's House

SEATED ON A STOOL BEFORE THE VANITY mirror, Mandisa peered at the reflection of her hazel-brown eyes, her broad flat nose stretched across the pale yellow skin of her face that she wished were darker, and *the* hair—the latest source of angst that disturbed the already fragile peace that existed between her and her mother.

A mixture of happiness and sadness flooded her insides. Happiness because she knew that at least one person, the person who she admired the most—her Aunt Njogona— would be pleased with her new do. But she was also saddened—made to feel ashamed because of what *it* supposedly signified. With her eyes held fixed on the coiled bumps, beeswax dancing in between the tight twisted half soon-to-be-matted hair, she could hear her mother from behind the bedroom door deliver a homily on the virtues of proper deportment.

"Get rid of *it!*" she said commandingly.

The *it* her mother wanted her to get rid of was the personification of vagrant marijuana smokers, of good-for-nothing lay-abouts—which was of course not what she wanted for her daughter. *It* was the identity badge of wayward miscreants and lumpen hormonal teenagers who were rebelling because they had nothing better to do. At least that was the prevailing idea at the time—an idea that was congruent with her mother's beliefs (which she spared no expense of repeating over and over and over again ever since Mandisa came home from the hairdresser's donning twists she never removed).

Sometimes, in response to her mother's droning, Mandisa would say, "Mamma, it's not how you see it. Kids like me are abandoning the system of mis-head-decaytion, discovering our own truths. We are finding ourselves. Plus, Aunt Njogona has beautiful dreadlocks and she doesn't do any of the things you say people with dread-locks do, does she?"

"Listen to me Mandisa," her mother would say in response. "That's how everybody else around here sees it. Having that hairstyle is calling unnecessary attention to yourself. It's even worst for Black boys to have dreadlocks and walk around with their facial hair unkempt. You're standing there telling me about finding yourself. Can't you do it some other way?"

Her mother's droning made her more depressed. It was point-less trying to reason with her. She would never approve. Mandisa sighed deeply. A mist of fog from her warm white breath settled coating the mirror before her as she sat studying what would in weeks become fuzzy, matted hair disheveled by wind, rain, sunlight, peppered with fragments of lint that had attached themselves to her golden hair ends. She felt a sense of freeness. Freedom from nights of eye-pulling, scalp-tearing braided extensions which was invariably followed by a tightly wrapped scarf fixing her freshly made cornrows in place in preparation for the next day. Freedom from the early morning rituals of, "I don't know what to do with my hair today."

Yes, in many ways, Mandisa's premature dreadlocks signaled for her freedom from the rules of conformity; it was her small celebra-tion of an example of beauty her Aunt Njogona embodied. When she left the salon the day after cutting her once straightened ends, replaced by her now kinky twisted roots, she smiled a dazzling smile as she looked off into the mirror before the exit sign and whispered quietly to herself, "Finally, I can be."

Now months later, she sat fingering her hair, toying with imaginings of what she would look like in a few years when her golden brown locks had grown and stretched down her back edging her buttocks. She thought of her Aunt Njogona. Her thoughts were disturbed by her mother's thundering voice outside her bedroom door.

She shuddered. With a shriek, she squeezed her eyes closed. She kept them closed until her mother's undulating voice slowly dissolved. Deep in the silence, she began to summon memories of the last summer spent at her Aunt Njogona's.

*

Njogona's voice carried with the magnanimity of a warrior but was balanced by an effervescent countenance. Her cherry lips would part into a generous chalk white smile that pulled even strangers toward her. She was short in stature but her thick matted hair scooped up in an oversized bun on her head made her appear taller. On any given day, she fluttered about the house in a delirium trying to get this task and that task done while whispers of patchouli fragrance wafted the air she left behind. Not today. Today was one of the few days when she rested long enough to let her freshly shampooed locks hang dry as she sat watching the scorched grass and the flowers below the porch bend languidly, welting in the sweltering July heat.

Mandisa watched closely as Aunt Njogona wrapped a towel around a few dampened locks while others fell in different directions about her nape and shoulders, the rest tracing a thick path down the middle of her back. Grayish-silver streaks peppered and coiled through the darker sections. They danced in and out of each lock as if someone were weaving a pattern for a straw basket through them.

Mandisa sat on the wooden steps of the front porch studying Njogona's mouth as it opened and closed over words that flowed bountifully from her thick lips. When she spoke, her eyebrows arched in excitement and her dark full eyelashes darted rapidly in a way that seemed to be in synchrony with her wildly gesticulating hands as she palmed rolled her locks and dug her fingers into the jar of Shea butter softening it between her finger tips all at the same time.

Mandisa's eyes travelled from the jar of shea butter, up towards her Aunt's silver-flecked hair where each lock was met with the requisite roll in between Njogona's soft moistened palms. She listened, swooning with excitement as Njogona narrated stories of rallies, marches, protests and organizing meetings where Black women in the neighbourhood gathered to discuss social issues.

Enchanted by Njogona's smell—a scent that stained Mandisa's

clothing weeks after she had returned to Toronto—she would lock herself in her bedroom for hours enveloped by the residue of Njogona's body oil. She longed to be back in the safety and comfort of her Aunt Njogona's home. There, the house was red-olent with the piquant fragrance of patchouli, lavender scented oils or sage burning unendingly in a metal plate in the centre of the dining table. There, she did not have to eat food left in the fridge that had to be microwaved because her mother was working double shift three days in a row—again. There, at Aunt Njogona's, Black folks walked proudly, wore dashikis and sported Afros, dreadlocks, braids and cornrows in their hair; they talked about going back to Africa, about loving Blackness and about the struggle for African liberation. There, she could ask questions, pose challenges to adults without being scolded or made to feel even more self-conscious about the efflorescent bumps on her chest—an insecurity that was magnified by her mother's stinging reminders that her pubescent parts did not give her license to say and do whatever she pleased. There, she met people who made her language and learning about politics, the music, the stories of Azania—the place where she was from—sound fascinating. There, the stories her Aunt Njogona told made her feel like back home was a place worth being proud of.

It was not that her mother did not have stories about apartheid or of organizing to protest the apartheid system. She did. Mandisa had heard her tell them once before when the pastor of The Latter Day Baptist Church at Oakwood and Vaughn asked her mother one day to speak to the congregation during a Sunday morning service when the church held a fundraiser to support the boycott, divestment sanction campaigns underway in parts of the city.

At the end of her talk, Mandisa's mother sat down hurriedly in the pew with her back braced firmly against the church bench. The three of them—Mandisa, her sister Nombie and her brother Thandiwe—looked at her with questioning eyes. It was Thandiwe (the youngest of the three) who unable to quell his aching curiosity, tugged at his mother's dress and asked whisperingly, "Mamma, how come you never told us any of this?" at which she shrugged and turned her gaze back towards the pulpit where the pastor stood preaching.

In her mother's house she was taught that the way to survive was to refrain from speaking Xhosa, to speak the English their father had drilled into them, to become Canadian. And so, her brother, who suffered the consequences of having the name Thandiwe and who was subject to ridicule from girls and boy's at school, who because he had a name that when shortened easily sounded like a girl's name in English, began hating his Xhosa name and instead resolved to using his Christian name—Oliver.

At Aunt Njogona's, her voluptuous shape, her large buttocks which seemed disproportionate to her tiny frame, her golden wooly tight curls, her name was envied and celebrated.

"Girl, you're a real African," her Aunt Njogona would say smilingly. "Not like us folks born in America. Uhh-uhh. Not like us. We're here in this place desperately searching, trying to recover fragments of ourselves scattered all about. You're genuine and that's a lot to be proud of."

Hearing those words Mandisa smiled shyly and looked down at her feet.

With one palm folded, Aunt Njogona cupped Mandisa's chin, tilted her face upwards, the other she would use to gently caress Mandisa's smooth cheeks as she reminded her to hold her head high.

When Mandisa opened her eyes, she was jolted by the still present voice of her mother thundering through the bedroom door.

"You had better take those things out. No respectable young lady wears her hair in dreadlocks. That's for hoodlums and thugs on the street corner. I swear to you Mandisa, you better take them out. Cuz if I have to, I am taking you straight to the barbers'."

Mandisa rose up quickly from her stool, rushed towards the door and turned the lock softly and slowly. She crouched with her knees propped up against her chin and her back braced against the door.

I'm a Black Girl

"MUMMY, LOOK, THE SUN IS WAKING UP." She stirs the sheets, nudges my shoulder and sways her legs back and forth under the covers. When I pretend not to hear her, she peels back the curtain slightly. A steady streak of incandescent sunlight splashes over my face.

"Damn it!" I mumble under my breath before covering my head to keep the sunlight out of my eyes. I fall back into sleep mode. She continues to duck and dive under and out of the sheets beside me. A cacophony of sounds in the distance: the roar of the city traffic ten floors below, cars honking a series of interminable honks, dogs barking as their owners take them for their early morning walks, sirens screaming, and wailing drunkards who had been hollering from the night before continue into the early morning pulling me out of my abysmal dream. I lay, now half awake, sunlight seeping in through my once darkened cavern of sleep.

Still groggy, peeling back the sheet a little I peek through half opened eyelids at my daughter kneeling upright in bed, her shoulders taut. I feel for my cell phone. It vibrates as I try to locate it.

It is 6:30 a.m. And even though I have grown accustomed to the early morning stirrings of my three-year-old alarm clock, I lay crippled by disbelief unable to fathom how it is that no matter how I had exhausted her the night before or how late I had put her to bed, she would awake and just like my cell phone, sound off an alarm at that precise hour each day.

"Okay, baby, okay," I say slowly opening my eyes. The curtains screech across the iron rod as she pulls them farther apart. She returns to where I am laying, jerks my shoulders and pries my eyelids open with her tiny fingers. I awake to a now unrestrained sunlight barreling through the neat part in the thick curtains my daughter just created.

In a high-pitched tone she repeats only this time yelling, "Mummy, wake up! The sun is awake and the moon is gone to sleep, time to get up! "

"Ma'at, Mummy's tired. Just a few more minutes, I just need a few more minutes, okay?" I say pleading with her.

She doesn't hear me. She tells me instead, "But Mummy, I want something to eat."

"Alright, alright. What do you want to eat for breakfast?" I ask even though I know she will say, "Sweet honey and peanut butter on bread and chocolate milk."

Now, having my full attention, she scampers off the bed, skips through the bedroom door, and twirls down the short hallway into the kitchen.

I slip out from under the covers, quickly tighten the robe about my waist and follow her.

Reaching into the cupboards, I pull out a jar of almond butter and a bottle of agave nectar. I spoon a dollop of almond butter, drizzle some agave nectar onto a slice of bread before spreading them both on slices of bread. I walk over to her small play table in the living room area where she sits waiting. I place the stainless steel plate before her with a glass of chocolate almond milk.

"A sandwich Mummy," she says doling out a command. "Squish it together like a sandwhich."

I fold the bread in half one side covering the other. She beams her approval.

Seated at my desk I open the laptop, click on iTunes and select a song from my reggae dancehall playlist. I open up the browser and go to my e-mail inbox.

The subject line of fifty unread messages flash across the screen in bolded black—a reminder of people I have yet to get back to. I close the browser, tilt my head and look off to the side where Ma'at sits. I watch as she frets bread edges before meticulously laying them out onto her silver plate in a series of triangular shapes. Our eyes meet. I smile. She smiles back sheepishly with her jaw stuffed. She chews, places her half-eaten almond butter sandwich down, hums, dances in her seat and taps her feet.

A fast beat, dancehall song starts to play. She rises up and the chair careens from under her legs on the floor.

She screams excitedly twirling towards me. "Look at me Mummy. Look. See me dancing," she continues with her hands at her side, waist twisting and hips grinding in an awkward circular motion.

"Ma'at," I ask smiling. "What are you doing?"

"I'm dancing Mummy. I'm dancing! Now its your turn to dance Mummy."

She marches toward me, pulls me up from the chair and screams, "You have to stand up Mummy!"

Bass pounds at the foot of the table. Vibrations travel, shaking pens, books, and bits of papers on my desk jump. The tiny desk lamp perched beside my laptop glides and jerks to the beat. I feel the hardwood floor quake beneath my feet as dancehall artiste Beenie Man's "Sim simma whose got di keys to ma bimma"[1] blasts through the speakers.

"Child, that's not how you whine. Do like so." I say crouching with my legs spread slightly apart demonstrating a smooth grinding motion.

She imitates, her waist moving rapidly off beat.

I laugh loudly at her ungainly hip movements.

"You're way too stiff Ma'at. Free up yu self gyal. Yu dance like a white girl," I say to her chuckling. She continues her awkward hip thrusting motion.

"No," she responds giggling. "I'm not a white girl, I'm a Black girl Mummy."

I stop sedated, my hands spread out to the side still suspended mid air from my half completed demonstration of *the butterfly* dance. I stare at her quietly, trying to understand whether she knew what she had just said. I wanted to stop the music and probe her. I wanted to explain how important that knowledge of self was.

Instead, I take her hands and pull her towards me. Lifting her to my chest and lowering her to the ground, laughter spills from her lips as I twirl her rapidly in the air.

Eventually dizzied, we collapse. Her juice stained TV blanket receives us as we meet with the floor. We lay panting heavily. I hear the music selection switch and Bob Marley and The Wailers' *Babylon System* fades in:

> *We refused to be what you wanted us to be*
> *We are who we are that's the way it's going to be*
> *If you don't know*
> *You can't educate us for no equal opportunities (Talking*
> *bout my freedom)*
> *Talking 'bout freedom, people, freedom and liberty*
> *Babylon system is a vampire*
> *Sucking the children day by day. Yeah*
> *Babylon system is a vampire (Vampire)*
> *Sucking the blood of the sufferer. Yeah*
> *Building church and university*
> *Deceiving the people continually....*

There lying on the blanket, the side of my head pressed up against my daughter's, I feel a strange feeling of happiness and relief overcome me. Reaching for my cell phone, I shoot off a text message to her village Aunties and Uncles. "You wouldn't believe what Ma'at just told me as we were dancing? I'm a Black girl! She tells me she's a Black girl. LOL!"

The phone vibrates almost immediately in my hand. A text message flashes across the display screen. "She's got it, no need to worry Mamma, our little girl has got it."

My heart flutters, my lips part into a faint smile. My mind dissolves melding with the sweet sounds of the Bob Marley as he wails on...

> *Tell the children the truth.*
> *Tell the children the truth.*

---

[1]Translation: Simmer, whose got the keys to my BMW?

Epilogue

HERstory is OURstory:
The Narrative of My Method

MY CELL PHONE CHIMES AS I EXIT the subway. I reach into my coat pocket and pull it out holding my gloved hand steadily. Blowing snow lifts my windswept locks and splatters them over my face. Slipping one glove off with my teeth, I peer into the "Rainey incoming text message" in the cell phone display. I slide my index finger across the touch screen and open the message:

"Dear God, got my daughter's report card the other day, and she had a crazy amount of 'lates to school'. I freaked out and sent an email to the teacher questioning … I had a meeting with him this morn, and he told me that I was aggressive. Am I?"

I text back: "Of course we're aggressive. We are women with lots of melanin in our skin. Lmao! There is an automatic scripting of our bodies that takes place once we attempt to assert our voice or challenge any unfair treatment. The actions we engage in on a daily basis are never seen as resistance; rather, they are understood as indicators of our 'inherent bestial emotions' (Johal, 2005, p. 282). You have to remember that, sis."

Seconds later, the phone chimes again in my hand: "Haha! He took issue with me saying that I said his lack of communication with me was an oversight and unacceptable. I thought he was going to cry."

"Cry? Really. I must say I never saw you as fitting the 'Aggressive Black Woman' stereotype. I better be scared of you from now on. LOL!"

Rainey texts back: "He told me that when he got my email, he couldn't teach and he hasn't been sleeping. I had no idea that I had that effect on people."

I write back: "Sounds like he's fishing for some stress leave from work. Either that, or he is about to lay some spurious harassment accusation to the school board. What a way to turn this around on you, eh? Anyways sis, pay him no mind. If you spend too much mental energy on this, you will drive yourself insane trying to figure out where you went wrong."

"So what are you doing now?"

"Just dropped my little one off at daycare. I'm heading back to the building to write now. Still trying to polish up the story from our transcribed conversation."

"Adwoa, you've been trying to make this story perfect for weeks now."

"Well, I admit I'm afraid of what you'll think about it. My insecurity. I just get really anxious when people read anything I write. I want to make sure it's perfect."

"Listen lady, it'll never be perfect. I wanna see it. Maybe I could give you some feedback. Why don't you pop by my apartment? I made red velvet cupcakes last night. We could share some over tea."

"Sounds good. Give me about fifteen minutes to run up to my place and get my laptop."

"Okay."

"All right. See you soon!"

I arrive on the fourth floor of our building at Rainey's apartment. I lift my hand to knock. The door swings open. Rainey props the door open with her feet and emerges holding a large laundry basket.

"Hey you! You're here already? I was just going downstairs to the laundry room," she says settling the basket down on the floor. "Your fifteen minutes usually turns into an hour. I thought I'd have some time to throw in another load."

"Not this time," I laugh. "I'm actually here in fifteen like I told you."

Rufus, Rainey's old German Sheppard, rushes to the door barking.

"Hush Rufus!" Rainey yells as she yanks his collar and drags him in between her legs and the laundry basket.

"Settle down now; it's only Adwoa."

Rufus whimpers and crouches down with his tail wagging.

"Good boy," she says patting his head.

"What's gotten into him today?" I ask.

"Well, some kids have been running back and forth on their way to the recreation room. What with the screaming and sounds of feet barreling down the hallway, I guess he's a little spooked. He probably thought you were one of the noisy brats," she chortles.

"Is there something going on in there today?" I ask as I peer down the hallway. I notice children floating in and out slamming the door behind them.

"I don't know," Rainey responds. "But there's always something going on in this building. "And," she continues, "Of course, as my luck would have it, I just happen to live on the floor where all the action takes place. Anyhow, come on in."

I pull out a chair and plop down around the dining table. Rainey bobs and weaves into the kitchen. Surfacing moments later, she plunks a cup of peppermint tea before me.

"Thanks, girl."

"No problem, I know how much you love peppermint tea."

"I sure do," I reply, clasping my hands around the large mug.

Rufus curls up under my legs near the foot of the table. Rainey returns to the dining room with two red velvet cupcakes swirled with cream cheese frosting and topped with pink and red sprinkles.

"Eh em. Check you out. Aren't you the Black Martha Stewart," I say teasingly.

"Aww. Stop. I like baking. It's therapeutic. Plus I had a bit of time on my hands, which is unusual, so I thought I would spend it with Taryn baking cupcakes.

"I hear ya."

"Anyhow, let's get down to the business of this story you wrote from our transcribed conversation."

"Okay," I say hesitantly. "Do you wanna take a couple minutes to read it over or should I read it to you?"

"Nah," she says. "I think it makes more sense if you read it out aloud."

"Well ... all right," I exhale and sigh heavily before continuing. "I titled the story 'The E(racing): Trapped in a Pigmentory Prison'."

I begin reading quickly, but with ease.

Ten minutes later, I look up from my computer to find Rainey, round-eyed, staring at me. She looks down at Rufus who sits with his front paws crossed on her lap eyeing her pitifully. He lowers his eyes as she reaches toward his face and palms his jaws. Rufus passes his tongue over his nose.

I watch as Rainey leans in closer and places her nose slightly against his slobbering wet nose.

"So, what do you think about the story?" I ask slowly bringing my teacup towards my lips.

She looks at me surreptitiously. "I like it. I do, " she repeats as if to reassure me even as I sense that she has some reservations.

A brief but intense silence follows before she speaks again. "But tell me something. We spent quite a long time talking and, uh, I mean there was so much in our conversation—why did you chose to create a story out of that particular memory?"

"I suppose I could have chosen to story some other memory, but honestly this one resonated with me because of my own experiences. In many ways that part of the transcript really spoke to my childhood spent struggling to escape the prison of my skin colour and hair. I also felt that if your story resonated with me, then, surely it was apt to speak to others about their lives (Bochner & Ellis, 2000)."

"I see," Rainy responds softly. "I am also wondering about the details. Well, I guess that's a bit unfair seeing that I really didn't give you a lot to work with right? I mean, I told you about being the only coloured girl in my school—how I used to get teased all the time—and that I would go home and try to rub the colour off my skin. In any case, I think it's fascinating that you were able to create this whole event from what was really a segment of our conversation. Even so, I wonder about the implication for truth in these types of projects."

She pauses and glares at me in frustration. "I am schooled in a different arena where rigor is critical. The academy tells us objective truth is the measure of research credibility. Not that I am negating the methodology or implying that it lacks rigor—I am not saying that at all. But I think for us to know that the research tools that we are using are good tools, we have to ask ourselves these questions. Don't we?" She turns to me looking for confirmation before asking, "Given that you had to fill in the details to make the story come alive, is the integrity of my story compromised?

What does that mean for representation? Can you really say that this is *my* story? I know I am being a bit of a pain right now. And I don't mean to, honestly."

"Not at all Rainey: these are really important questions."

"Well," she continues. "The trouble for me is this: let's say in writing my story you change the objects in the room. Does it still make it my story? Say you offered a description of the furniture—a chair for instance—as being, I don't know, a leather couch when really it was an old wooden chair." She continues laughing, "I know, I know. It seems so trivial, but what if, for example, I actually showered in a bath pan in the backyard and not in a bathtub inside a house as you have depicted in the story? What if in the reconfiguring of the details you present me as having grown up middle class when the reality is I grew up in a working class home? How can we then say that this is good research if we do not guard against these misgivings?"

"Hmm." I pause to think before rephrasing her question out loud, "So I think you are asking me if the details matter in my understanding of good research?"

She nods in agreement.

A few seconds pass before I am able to respond.

"These are the very concerns with which many narrative researchers struggle. The issue of whether narrative researchers through the creation of plot, dialogue, and scene setting merely falsify, distort or fictionalize our participants' lived experiences has been front and centre of these discussions (Banks & Banks, 1998; Bochner et al., 1997; Bochner, 2001; Bochner 2002; Bochner & Ellis, 2002; Freeman, 1998; MacIntyre, 1981; Mink, 1969-1970). While we ought to be concerned about these possibilities, Bochner (2002) reminds us that storied representation is not 'a neutral attempt to mirror the facts of one's life' (p. 86). Rather, our story's purpose is to tease out 'the significance of meaning of one's experiences' (Bochner, 2002, p. 87). Through the medium of the creative imagination, narrative researchers are able to order, make sense of, and give significance to often fragmented recollections of the past (Bochner, 2002, citing Crites, 1971). Narrative devices such as dramatic arcs, setting and characterization, says Ungar (2011), serve as an interpretive schema that facilitates an understanding of our lived experiences 'as more than a series of disjointed temporal events' (p. 292). Through storying—defined as 'the process of structuring experiences into stories' (Banks-Wallace, 2002, p. 141)—researchers are able to communicate in a structured, creative, evocative and accessible form the understandings and insights we glean from the information relayed to us by participants (Banks & Banks, 1998; Berger & Quinney, 2005). The power of story resides in its ability to both engage and invite readers into the storied moment while creating a deliberate point of view from which we understand the events. While this may seem like a curious retelling to some, I understand it as a deliberate act that makes explicit the role of interoperation in our storied lives."[1]

Her face is pregnant with doubt. Her once perfectly arched eyebrows are now furrowed. I encounter momentary paralysis realizing that she is not convinced. I sit in a rapture of silence thinking about this ethical conundrum. How do I open up new understandings and possibilities for engaging in storymaking research (Banks & Banks, 1998) in a way that honours the core values of human dignity and allows for voice without inflicting epistemological violence? Is it possible to dislodge positivist paradigms without enacting the very disempowering research methodologies such approaches are often charged with? Through Rainey's questioning, I am confronted with the challenge of navigating the ethical issues that are inherent in narrative representations (Bochner & Ellis, 2000). The problematics of my assumed interpretive authority (Borland, 1991) have become more real.[2] I reflect further on Blaufuss (2007) who tells me that the relationship between researcher and research participants is one wherein the narrative researcher wields tremendous power in selecting and reconstructing stories shared in the initial dialogical engagements. Though I am not sure how or whether I can assuage all ethical concerns raised by Rainey, I know it is particularly important that I address her concerns given the nature of my research, and that I am representing the lives of women from a historically marginalized group. My dilemma becomes all the more complex because I, a scholar and academic researcher of African descent, know all too well that my ancestors, like many other Indigenous peoples share a history of epistemological violence wrought by colonizing research methodologies (Smith, 2012).

My discomfort grows the more I become aware of my competing subjectivities—the possibility of the 'oppressor planted deep within' (Lorde, 1984/2007, p. 123) my body—a body positioned historically as the 'Other'. How do I negotiate my 'outsider within' researcher status (Collins, 1991)? Even as I know that all research is subjective and value-laden (Blaufauss, 2007; Bochner & Ellis, 2000; Borland, 1991; Moen, 1997), I also understand that the implications of not giving voice to Rainey's objections is that I could reproduce the silencing, the alienation, the violence, the exploitative tendencies of European colonial research practices (Smith, 2012).

Not having answers, I make another attempt to honour Rainey's voice. I do so by going back to my roots—storytelling.

The damp silence looms heavier. It is finally broken when I ask, "Rainey, may I share with you a Jamaican Anancy[3] folk story that I tell my daughter before bed?"

She nods. "Yeah. Sure."

"The story is called "Anancy and Common Sense."[4] I usually tell it to her in the Jamaican language."

She winces.

"Don't look so worried," I say before continuing. "Of course, I am going to have to tell it to you in English so you'll understand. Some of the words just don't translate in English but I'll do my best, okay?"

She nods, "All right. That works for me."

Once upon a time Anancy got this idea that he could collect all the common sense in the world and keep it to himself. That way he could get a lot of money and power because, everybody would come to him with their troubles and he would charge them a high price for advice. So, Anancy started out to collect all the common sense he could find and put it in a big calabash . When he searched and searched and could not find any more common sense, Anancy decided to hide the calabash filled with common sense in the top of the tallest tree in the village where no one else could reach it.

Anancy then tied a rope around the neck of the calabash and attached the calabash to his stomach. After which, he attempted to climb the tree. In trying to climb, Anancy realized that he couldn't make it up the tree where he wanted to hide the calabash. Each time he would jump onto the tree, he would fall down. Even still, Anancy kept on trying. After hours and numerous attempts he suddenly heard a little girl's voice calling out to him at the foot of the tree: 'Anancy you are so foolish. Don't you know that if you want to climb the tree, it's best to put the calabash on your back? That way you can move up the tree easier.'

Anancy looked down in shock at the little girl standing at the tree's stump. He was quite upset to hear that big piece of common sense come out of the mouth of such a little girl. He was certain that he had collected all the common sense and that there was no more left in the world. Enraged, Anancy yanked the calabash from around his neck and threw it to the ground. The calabash broke into pieces and all the common sense floated and scattered all over the world. And from that day onwards, everybody got a little bit of common sense.

When I stop speaking, Rainey looks at me, and says, "Okay, Adwoa. I know you're trying to make a point here so why did you tell me that story?"

"Well, when I share this story with my daughter, I don't always tell her the story the same way. For example, sometimes I change the child's gender depending on the message I am consciously trying to impart to my daughter. Sometimes I'll also change elements of the story to fit the Canadian context because I know that stories, much like the cultural space they emanate from, are always in flux (Ungar, 2011). The storytelling event is therefore influenced by my subjectivity and agenda as a storyteller as well as my understanding of the socio-cultural terrain.

"I (re)present the Anancy story in multiple ways partly because I grew up hearing variants of this same story. I have heard one version where the calabash simply falls off Anancy's back and breaks open as he climbs. In that version, there is no one at the bottom of the tree calling out to Anancy. I also remember hearing another adaptation where the dialogue changes significantly. I am saying all this to make transparent my belief that stories as knowledge is transient. Consider for a minute if you and I sat right here, observed an event or were told a story, and someone later asked us to write about what we saw or heard. Do you think we'd render the story in the exact same way?"

"I am not so sure that we would," she responds.

"Neither am I. I guess the point I am trying to make in telling you this Anancy story is that the changes in the details don't detract from the central message that Anancy wanted to hoard all the knowledge and that he failed at doing so. Neither do the changes take away from the underlying socio-cultural lessons that are embedded in this particular folk story. Changing the details, though, can allow me as storyteller to reach particular audiences in specific contexts for particular reasons. Indigenous scholar and writer Thomas King, supports this notion when he states that '[we are] merely retelling the same stories in different patterns' (2003, p. 2). From an indigenous perspective, then, it is the lesson that matters—not so much whether the story is told exactly as it happened or related the same way each time it is told.

"Ellis & Bochner (2000) suggests that we ask ourselves two key questions: first, does the lesson, experience, or emotion, resonate in a way that helps readers understand the intent; and can someone who is not present in that lived experience glean insight into the larger meaning of the story? Similarly, they argue, that the usefulness of the story resides in inspiring conversation and engendering critical reflection from its audiences."

Still looking doubtful, Rainey says, "Now that I think about it, that makes a bit of sense. I mean, in my interpretation, that Anancy story spoke to the wisdom of the child. I understand it to mean that the child in effect shatters the dominant perception that you have to be older to be wiser or to possess knowledge."

"Oh, wow!" I pipe in. "There's another important interpretation. For me, this Anancy folktale reinforces a knowing that is central to indigenous ontologies: that is, no one person can own stories. Said another way, the folktale reinforces the communal aspect of indigenous knowledge systems. In this folktale, Anancy wanted to do what seems natural for us to do when we ask: 'Is this my story?' What the child at the bottom of the tree reminds us is that your story is our story. In other words, one individual story is part of a larger collective cultural story. In indigenous ontologies, stories are our knowledges. Margaret Kovach (2009) echoes this sentiment when she states that in indigenous worldviews, 'knowledge and story are inseparable' (p. 98). Our knowledges live by being shared, retold and recreated. It is in the retelling, in the recreating, that knowledges grow and remain part of our collective historical memory. Our stories do not survive the generations by being bottled up, fixed in time or place, and possessed by one person. Do you understand?"

She nods and says, "Yeah, I get it."

"On the question of 'truth', I think our different interpretations of this one Anancy folktale is very telling. Not only does it shatter any notion that there is a single 'truth' available to social science researchers; it also reinforces the notion that 'truth is contested and polyvocal' (Berger & Quinny, 2005, p. 3). Moen eloquently troubles the notion that there is a static truth when he states, '[t]here is no single, dominant or static reality but, rather, a number of realities that are constructed in the process of interactions and dialogues. Human knowledge of the world is thus relative. It is dependent on the individual's past and present experiences, her or his values, the people the stories are being told to (the addressees), and when and where they are being told' (Moen, 2006, p. 60 citing Bhaktin, 1986).

"In writing the story, "The Erace(ing): Trapped in a Pigmentory Prison," I present to audiences one creative interpretation or rendering of that storied moment in your life. Of course there are other interpretations, other representations that can be offered up. However, as Ungar reminds us, '[t]he power of [story] isn't that it tells truth, but that it forces us to acknowledge that all truths coexists [and] that others have different ways of understanding and making sense of the world' (Ungar, 2011, p. 293).

The different renderings and interpretations of *Anancy and Common Sense* only reinforce the above perspective, reminding us that, "every story is partial and situated" (Ellis & Bochner, 2000, p. 750)."

"Adwoa," she says. "What you are telling me runs completely counter to what I have been taught constitutes valid research."

"Yeah, I know. This is why I want to encourage readers to approach narrative research inquiries using a different analytical toolkit. This is particularly important when judging narrative

representations based on the lived experiences of African de-
scended peoples. You have to use different measures of research
goodness (Cole & Knowles, 2008) consistent with the ways in
which Afro-indigenous peoples come to know and understand
themselves in relation to the world. You ask about measures of
research goodness? Well, narrative methodology rejects the logic
of empiricism, objectivism and positivism and instead advances an
alternative way of knowing consistent with indigenous research
paradigms. It presents knowledge in an evocative, emotionally
engaging way that embraces creativity, subjectivity and is open to
multiple interpretations."

A brief pause follows before I continue. "Now, this is not to say
that as a researcher-turned-creative-writer I don't need details. The
more details I get from co-participants, the easier it is for me to write
a story that reflects as closely as possible the lived experience. But
we need to realize that it is impossible to capture an individual's
experience exactly the way it was lived. Even so, I try my best to
achieve as high level of 'authenticity' as is possible. This is why I go
back to the source of the recreated stories —I talk to participants
like your self. In doing this, I am performing what Ellis & Bochner
(2000) calls a 'reliability check' of sorts. Doing so, will allow for
the opening up space for co-participants to exchange ideas and
engage in discussions that tease out conflicting meanings and varying
interpretations of the final storied representation (Borland, 1991).
Going back to the sources that inspire our storying also signals to
readers that as researchers we are holding ourselves accountable
and acknowledging any 'factual distortions [or] contingencies'
(Bochner, 2002, p. 86) that may arise.

Even so, the challenge here is that many of us cannot or do not
want to remember. Even as we may recall significant life changing
parts of our experiences, we may not recall the specifics: whether the
chair was red or green, the weather on that day or what someone
might have said to us verbatim. In other instances, the memory
may be too painful to relive that we subconsciously tuck away
the details for fear of reopening wounds. What does the narrative
researcher do when confronted with this other ethical dilemma?
We certainly should not push participants to revisit what may have
been traumatic experiences by demanding more details to pacify

concerns that our creative representations are indeed 'truthful' or 'factual'. As researchers we have an ethical obligation to our participants. As such, we should always be concerned about the material impact our initial inquiries and subsequent representations may have on living participants (Bochner, 2002; Borderland, 1991). As a researcher from a historically marginalized group, I must be particularly sensitive to the fact that I bring into these dialogical engagements an understanding of the epistemological and psychological trauma that such research approaches inflict on formerly colonized peoples (Smith, 2012). I would rather allow room for using my creative imagination later on. My sense is that what matters is whether the heart of the story is still there."

"I guess that's really what matters, eh?" Rainey asks.

"Yup," I reply. " I would like to think that that's all that matters."

---

[1] I would like to acknowledge Ellyn Lyle for lending her insight on this point and for her careful edits of earlier drafts of this section.

[2] Borland (1991) takes up this issue of privileging interpretive authority in the context of feminist research, arguing that interpretive authority permeates all research. Similarly, Ungar (2011) tells us that "all writing has an author handily making sense of the world through his or her own words" (p. 295). Consistent with these perspectives, here I operate from the premise that knowledge production is not a neutral undertaking. Rather, knowledge production is highly political with its own inherent power relations. If we view narrative as a form of knowledge production, narrative researchers then have power. We come to our research with the power to filter, sort, order and represent lives (Blaufuss, 2007; Bochner & Ellis, 2000; Daya & Lau, 2007; Ungar, 2011). While this is so, we must also recognize that it is the exercise of and not the mere existence of that interpretive power that could result in exploitative or abusive power relationships in research. The cogent issue becomes how to value researcher interpretive frameworks and perspectives while honoring the interpretive lenses participants like Rainey bring to our storied representations. Narrative scholars suggest that one way forward in negotiating this power is to go back to the source that inspires our creative storying. These scholars urge us to include as much as possible our participants' perspectives and provide space in our narrative representations to engage in reflexivity, to hold ourselves accountable and to be

conscious of these unequal power dynamics (Bochner and Ellis, 2002; Borland, 1991; Ungar, 2011). My exchange here with Rainey is my attempt at making transparent the tensions in researcher interpretive authority of which Borland (1991) speaks. Importantly, our exchange provides space for challenging our interpretive framings of participant's lived experiences.

[3]Anancy and his stories are thought to have travelled with Africans taken into captivity and brought across the transatlantic ocean to the Americas during the period of European enslavement. In the context of plantation slavery, the folk icon Anancy (and the stories named after him) became a vehicle for cultural, psychological and physical resistance and survival. Today, Anancy stories are told as part of the folk cultural tradition in Jamaica. For Afro-Caribbean peoples in particular, Anancy folk tales represent a vital link to our African ancestry (Marshall, 2001). In the context of my conversation with Rainey, this Anancy folk tale serves an even more important function. It becomes the interpretive framework that facilitates critical reflection on conceptions of "truth" from an indigenous standpoint. Through unpacking the meaning of this Anancy folk story, both Rainey and I become engaged in what Archibald (2001) calls "storywork". As a researcher, I am forced to use storywork "to think deeply and to reflect upon [my] actions and [Rainey's] reactions" (p. 1) as well as the larger social implications of the two types of stories (personal and cultural/mythical stories) told here (See Kovach, 2009 for a discussion of the difference between personal and cultural stories).

[4]The story "Anancy an Common Sense" was taken from Bennet's (1979) collection *Anancy and Miss Lou.*

Glossary of Words

Akete drum: a high-pitched drum

Nyame: is the sky god of the Ashanti and Akan people of Ghana

Duppy: a ghostlike creature in Caribbean folklore, believed to have the capability of harming or overpowering humans; a ghost or spirit

Obeah: an African religious tradition practiced in Jamaica that is usually classified as sorcery or Black magic

Whine: this word appears in many languages in the Caribbean region and is a literal reinvention of the word "wind." When used in the context of the dancehall in Jamaica, it describes a circular (sometimes) seductive movement of the waist and hips

Ackee: the national fruit of Jamaica, consisting of a spongy, red skin with fleshy yellow pods and black seeds inside

Cowitch: a wild bush that causes itching and swelling of the skin

Calabash: a smooth, large hard-shelled gourd use as a drinking and eating utensil

Rastafari: a religious, spiritual and political order that is based on African philosophy and traditions. A Rastafarian therefore is a person who holds to beliefs centred on this philosophy.

Adinkra Symbols:
Their Meaning and Significance

Adinkra is a language system that has been used for centuries by the Akan of West Africa in Ghana. In Akan cosmology, the world is made up of two realms: the world of the physical (the world of the living) and the nonphysical (spiritual world). Blay (2008) tells us that both worlds compliment each other and every living creature is thought to transition between these two realms through the cycle of birth, puberty, marriage, physical death and rebirth. Each symbol contains its own narrative about the Akan people and their relationship to land, the environment and the ancestors.

The reader will notice that I have woven some of these symbols into each storied chapter. The symbols, though aesthetically appealing, lend more than just aesthetic consistency to the book. Importantly, they speak to the educative possibilities of the work. Each Adinkra has pedagogical significance and connects to the theme of the chapters as well as to the larger story on African maternal pedagogies.

As a unique structured language system, Adinkra (similar to the Anancy stories) serves as a medium for the articulation of Afro-indigenous cultural knowledges and worldviews. As a system of communication, the symbols serve an important storytelling function in terms of conveying messages about Akan cosmological principles, cultural values and beliefs. Some of their messages have been adopted by Africans the world over and continue to be used as an expression of our collective historical memory. Below is a list with meanings of select Adinkra symbols used throughout this work:

Throughout the book:
Ananse Ntontan: "Spider web." Anancy represents the symbol of wisdom, creativity, and the complexities of life.

Chapter 1:
Owua Atwede: "The ladder of death or symbol of mortality." It serves as a reminder of the transitory nature of existence in this world and of the imperative to live a good life to be a worthy soul in the afterlife.

Chapter 2:
Boa Me Na Me Mmoa Wo: "Help me and let me help you". This symbolizes cooperation and interdependence.

Chapter 3:
Duafe: "The wooden comb". This is the symbol of beauty (specifically feminine beauty).

Chapter 4:
Aya: "Defiance, endurance, resourcefulness." The fern is a hardy plant that can grow in difficult places. An individual who wears this symbol is known to have endured many adversities and outlasted much difficulty.

Chapter 5:
Sankofa: "Return and get it." This symbol speaks to the importance of learning and recovering from the past.

Bibliography

Anatol, G. L. (2002). Speaking mother tongues the role of language in Jamaica Kincaid's: The autobiography of my mother. *Callaloo,* 25(3), 938-953.

Anderson, I., & Cundall, F. (1910/1927). *Jamaican proverbs and saying: Collected and classified according to subjects.* London, UK: Published for the Institute of Jamaica by the West Indies committee.

Banks-Wallace, J. (1998). Emancipatory potential of storytelling in a group. *Journal of Nursing Scholarship,* 30 (1), 17-22.

Banks, A., & Banks, S. (Eds.) (1998) *Fiction & social research: By ice or fire* (pp. 137-146). Walnut Creek, CA: AltaMira Press.

Bell, D. (1987). *And we will not be saved: The elusive quest for racial justice.* New York: Basic Books.

Bell-Scott, P. et al., (Eds.) (1993). *Double stitch: Black women write about mothers and daughters.* New York: HarperPerennial.

Bennet, L. (1979). *Anancy and miss lou.* Kingston, Jamaica: Sangster's Book Store Ltd.

Berger, J. & Quinney, R. (2005). *Storytelling sociology: Narrative as social inquiry.* Boulder, CO: Lynne Rienner Publishers.

Bernard, C., & Bernard, W. T. (1998). Passing the torch: A mother and daughter reflect on their experiences across generations. *Canadian Woman Studies/les cahiers de la femme,* 18(2), 46-51.

Bernard, C., Bernard, W. T., Epko, C., Enang, J., Joseph, B., & Wane, N. (2000). "She who teaches learns" othermothering in the academy: A dialogue among african canadian and african caribbean students and faculty. *Journal of the Association for*

Research on Mothering, 2(2), 66-84.

Blay, Y. A. (2008a). All the Africans' are men, all the "sistas" are "American", but some of us resists: Realizing african feminism(s) as an africological research methodology. *The Journal of Pan African Studies*, 2, 58-73.

Blay, Y. A. (2008b). Adinkra Symbols. In Molefi K. Asante and Ama Mazama (Eds.) *Encyclopedia of African religion* (pp. 8-11). Thousand Oaks, CA: Sage. Sage Reference Online. Available from http://sageereference.com.myaccess.library.utoronto.ca/view/africanreligion/n7.xml?rskey=X6Ma1F&result=1&q=adinkra#entrycitation. Accessed 7 Feb, 2012.

Bochner, A. P. (1985). Perspectives on inquiry: Representation, conversation, and reflection. In M. Knapp & G. R. Miller (Eds.), *Handbook of interpersonal communication* (pp. 27-58). Thousand Oaks, CA: Sage Publications.

Bochner, A. P., & Ellis, C. (1992). Personal narrative as a social approach to interpersonal communication. *Communication Theory*, 2, 165-172.

Bochner, A. P. (1994). Perspectives on Inquiry II: Theories and stories. In M. Knapp & G. R. Miller (Eds.), *Handbook of interpersonal communication* (2nd ed.) (pp. 21-41). Thousand Oaks, CA: Sage Publications.

Bochner, A. P. (1997). It's about time: Narrative and the divided self. *Qualitative Inquiry*, 3, 418-438.

Bochner, A. (2000). Criteria against ourselves. *Qualitative Inquiry*, 6, 266-272.

Bochner, A. P. (2001). Narrative's virtues. *Qualitative inquiry*, 7, 131-157.

Bochner, A. P. (2002). Perspectives on Inquiry III: The moral of stories. In M. Knapp & G. R. Miller (Eds.), *Handbook of interpersonal communication* (3rd ed.) (pp. 73-101). Thousand Oaks, CA: Sage Publications.

Boylorn, R. M. (2011a). Black kids (B.K.) Stories: Talking (about) race outside the classroom. *Cultural Studies/Critical Methodologies*, 11 (1), 59-70.

Boylorn, R. M. (2011b). Gray or for coloured girls who are tired of chasing rainbows: Race and reflexivity. *Cultural Studies/Critical Methodologies*, 11 (2), 178-186.

Byrd, D.L. (2011). Reflections on maternal/feminist service-learning pedagogy. In Deborah Lea Byrd and F. J. Green (Eds.), *Maternal pedagogies inside and outside the classroom* (pp. 135-156) Toronto, ON: Demeter Press.

Charles, C.A.D. (2009). Skin bleachers' representations of skin color in Jamaica. *Journal of Black Studies*, 40 (2), 153-170.

Cole, A. L., & Knowles, J. G. (2001). *Lives in context: The art of life history research*. Walnut Creek, CA: Altamira Press.

Cole, A. L., & Knowles, J. G. (Eds.) (2008a). (Eds.). *Handbook of the arts in qualitative research: Perspectives, methodologies, examples and issues*. Thousand Oaks, CA: Sage Publications.

Cole, A.L., & Knowles, J.G. (2008b). Arts-informed research. In A.L. Cole and J.G. Knowles (Eds.), *Handbook of the arts in qualitative research: Perspectives, methodologies, examples and issues* (pp. 55-70). Thousand Oaks, CA: Sage Publications.

Collins, P. H. (1986). Learning from the outsider within: The sociological significance of black feminist thought, *Social Problems*, 33(6), S14-S32.

Collins, P. H. (1987). The meaning of motherhood in black culture and black mother-daughter relationships. *Sage*, 4(2), 3-10.

Collins, P.H. (1994). Shifting the centre: Race, class and feminist theorizing about motherhood. *Mothering: ideology, experience, and agency* (pp. 45-65). In Evelyn Nakano Glenn, Grace Chang, and Linda Rennie Forcey. (Eds.), New York: Routledge.

Collins, P. H. (1998). *Fighting words: Black women and research for social justice*. Minneapolis, MN: University of Minnesota Press.

Collins, P. H. (2000a). Black women and motherhood. In P. Hill Collins (Ed.), *Black feminist thought* (Rev 10th anniversary ed., pp. 115-137). New York: Routledge.

Collins, P.H. (2000b). *Black feminist thought: Knowledge, consciousness, and the politics of empowerment*. (Rev 10th anniversary ed.). New York: Routledge.

Collins, P.H. (2007). The meaning of motherhood in black culture and mother-daughter relationships. In A. O'Reilly (Ed.), *Maternal theory essential readings* (pp. 274-289). Toronto, ON: Demeter Press.

Complete lyrics of Bob Marley: Songs of freedom. New York: Omnibus Press.

Crenshaw, K., Gotanda, N., Peller, G., & Thomas, K. (Eds.) (1995). *Critical race theory: The key writings that formed the movement.* New York, NY: New Press.

Crites, S. (1971). The narrative quality of experience. *Journal of the American Academy of Religion*, 39, 291-311.

Crites, S. (1971). Storytime: Recollecting the past and projecting the future. In T. Sarbin (Ed.), *Narrative psychology: The storied nature of human conduct* (pp. 152-173). New York: Praeger.

Cundall, F., & Anderson, I. (1972). *Jamaica proverbs and sayings.* Shannon, Ireland: Irish University Press.

Dance, D. (1985). *Folklore from contemporary Jamaicans.* Tennessee: University of Tennessee Press.

Daniel, B. (2005). Researching African Canadian women. In G. J. S. Dei & G. S. Johal (Eds.), *Critical issues in anti-racist research methodologies* (pp. 54-78). New York: Peter Lang.

Dei, G. J. S. (1990). Indigenous knowledge and economic production: The food crop cultivation, preservation and storage methods of a West-African rural community. *Ecology of food and nutrition* 24(1),1-20.

Dei, G. J. S. (1993). Indigenous african knowledge systems. *Tropical Geography*, 14 (1), 28-41.

Dei, G. J. S. (1994a). Creating reality and understanding: The relevance of indigenous African worldviews. Invitational address read at the Black History Month Celebration, Vancouver, B.C.

Dei, G. J. S. (1994b). Afrocentricity: A cornerstone of pedagogy. *Anthropology & Education Quarterly* 25(1), 3-28.

Dei, G. J. S .(2000a). Rethinking the role of indingeous knowledges in the academy. *International Journal of Inclusive Education*, 4(2), 111-132.

Dei, G. J. S., Hall, B. L., & Rosenberg, D. G. (2000b). (Eds.). *Indigenous knowledges in the global contexts: Multiple readings of our world.* Toronto: OISE/UT book published in association with University of Toronto Press.

Dei, G. J. S., Hall, B. L., & Rosenberg, D. G. (2000b). Introduction. In Dei G. J. S., Hall B. L. and Rosenberg D. G. (Eds.), *Indigenous knowledges in global contexts: Multiple readings of our world* (pp. 3-20). Toronto: OISE/UT book published in association with University of Toronto Press.

Dei, G. J. S. (2000b). African development: The relevance and implications of 'indigenousness'. In Dei G. J. S., Hall B. L. and Rosenberg D. G. (Eds.), *Indigenous knowledges in global contexts: Multiple readings of our world* (pp. 70-86). Toronto: OISE/UT book published in association with University of Toronto Press.

Dei, G. J. S. (2004). *Emancipationist thoughts and development: The possibilities of African indigenous knowledge in the academy.* Unpublished manuscript.

Dei, G. J. S., & Asgharzadeh, A. (2006). Indigenous knowledge and globalization: An african perspective. In A. A. Abdi, K. P. Puplampu & G. J. S. Dei (Eds.), *African education and globalization: Critical perspectives* (pp. 53-77). Lanham: Lexington Books.

Delgado, R. (1989). Storytelling for oppositionalists and others: A plea for narrative. *Michigan Law Review*, 87, 2411-2441.

Delgado, R. (1995). *Critical race theory: The cutting edge*. Philadelphia, PA: Temple University Press.

Duncan, C. B. (2005). Black women and mothering in contemporary cinematic science fiction. *Journal of the Association for Research on Mothering*, 5(1), 45-52.

Dundee, A. (1996). Metafolklore and oral literary vriticism. *The Monist*, 60: 505-516.

Donnell, A., & Lawson Welsh, S. (1996). *The Routledge reader in Caribbean literature*. New York: Routledge.

Edwards, A. (2000). Community mothering: The relationship between mothering and the community work of Black women. *Journal of the Association for Research on Mothering*, 2(2), 66-84.

Egan, K. (1995). Narrative and learning: A voyage of implications, (pp 116-125), in H. McEwan & K. Egan (Eds). *Narrative in teaching, learning, and research*. New York: Teachers College Press.

Ellis, C. (1991a). Emotional sociology. In N. K. Denzin (Ed.), *Studies in symbolic interaction: A research annual* (Vol. 12, pp. 123-145. Greenwhich, CT: JAI.

Ellis, C. (1991b). Sociological introspection and emotional experience. *Symbolic Interaction*, 14, 23-50.

Ellis, C. & Bochner, A.P. (1992). Telling and performing true stories: The constraints of choice in abortion. In C. Ellis & M.G. Flaherty (Eds), *Investigating subjectivity: Research on lived experience* (pp. 79-101). Newbury Park, CA: Sage.

Ellis, C. (1993). "There are survivors": Telling a story of sudden death. *Sociological Quarterly*, 34, 711-730.

Ellis, C. (1995a). *Final negotiations: A story of love, loss, and chronic illness*. Philadelphia, PA: Temple University Press.

Ellis, C. (1995b). Emotional and ethical quagmires in returning to the field. *Journal of Contemporary Ethnography*, 24, 711-713.

Ellis, C. (1995c). The other side of the fence: Seeing black and white in a small, southern town, *Qualitative Inquiry*, 1, 147-167.

Ellis, C. (1995d). Speaking of dying: An ethnographic short story. *Symbolic Interaction*, 18, 73-81.

Ellis, C., & Bochner, A. (1996a). *Composing ethnography: Alternative forms of qualitative writing*. Walnut Creek, CA: AltaMira.

Ellis, C., & Bochner, A. (1996b). Taking ethnography into the twenty-first century [Special Issue]. *Journal of Contemporary Ethnography*, 25 (1).

Ellis, C. (1997). Evocative autoethnography: Writing emotionally about our lives. In W. G. Tierney & Y. S. Lincoln (Eds.), *Representation and text: Re-framing the narrative voice* (pp. 115-142). Albany, NY: SUNY.

Ellis, C. (1998a). Exploring loss through autoethnographic inquiry: Autoethnographic stories, co-constructed narratives, and interactive interviews. In J. H. Harvey (Ed.), *Perspectives on loss: A sourcebook* (pp. 49-62). Philadelphia, PA: Taylor & Francis.

Ellis, C., & Bochner, A. (1999). Which way to turn? *Journal of Contemporary Ethnography*, 28, 485-499.

Ellis, C., & Bochner, A. (2000). Autoethnography, personal narrative, reflexivity: Reseacher as subject. In N. Denzin & Y. Lincoln (Eds.), *Handbook of qualitative research* (2nd ed., pp. 733-768). Thousand Oaks, CA: Sage.

Ellis, C. & Berger, L. (2001a). Their story, my story, our story: Including the researcher's experience in interview research. In J. Gubrium & J. Holstein (Eds.), *Handbook of interview research* (pp. 849-875). Thousand Oaks, CA: Sage.

Ellis, C. (2001). With mother/with child: A true story. *Qualitative Inquiry*, 7, 598-616.

Ellis, C. & Flemons, D. (2002). High noon: A "fictional" dialogue. In A. P. Bochner & C. Ellis (Eds.), *Ethnographically speaking:*

Autoethnography, literature, and aesthetics (pp. 344-356). Walnut Creek, CA: AltaMira.

Ellis, C., & Bochner, A. (2006). Analyzing analytic autoethnography: An autopsy. *Journal of Contemporary Ethnography, 35,* 429-449.

Ellis, C. (2007). 'I just want to tell MY story': Mentoring students about relational ethics in writing about intimate others. In N. K. Denzin & M. Giardina (Eds.), *Ethical futures in qualitative research: Decolonizing the politics of knowledge* (pp. 209-228). Walnut Creek, CA: Left Coast Press.

Ellis, C., Bochner, A., Denzin, N., Lincoln, Y, Morse, J., Pelias, R, & Richardson, L. (2007). Talking and thinking about qualitative research. In N. K. Denzin & M. D. Giardina. *Ethical futures in qualitative research: Decolonizing the politics of knowledge* (pp. 229-267). Oxford, UK: Berg Publishers.

Ellis, C. (2009). Talking across fences. In C. Ellis (Ed.) *Revision: Autoethnographic reflections on life and work* (pp. 35-59). Walnut Creek, CA: Left Coast Press Inc.

Fanon, F. (1967). *Black skin, white mask.* New York: Grove Press.

Freire, P. (2009). *Pedagogy of the oppressed* (30th anniversary Ed.) New York: Continuum International Publishing Group Inc.

Freeman, M. (1998). Experience, narrative, and the relation between them. *Narrative inquiry, 8,* 455-466.

Green, F.J. (2004). Feminist mothers: Successfully negotiating the tension between motherhood as 'institution' and 'experience'. In A. O'Reilly (Ed.), *From motherhood to mothering: The legacy of Adrienne Rich's of woman born* (pp. 125-136) Albany, NY: SUNY.

Green, F.J. (2006). Developing a feminist motherline: Reflections on a decade of feminist parenting. *Journal of the Association for Research on Mothering, 8* (1&2) 7-20.

Green, F.J. (2009). *Feminist mothering in theory and practice, 1985-1995.* Lewiston, NY: The Edwin Mullen Press.

Green, F. J. (2011). Feminist maternal pedagogies: Inside and Outside the Classroom. In Deborah Lea Byrd and F. J. Green (Eds.), *Maternal pedagogies inside and outside the classroom* (pp. 197-207) Toronto: Demeter Press.

hooks, b. (1981). *Ain't I a woman?: Black women and feminism.* Boston, MA: South End Press.

hooks, b. (1992). *Black looks: race and representation.* Boston, MA: South End Press.

hooks, b. (1994). Theory as Liberatory practice. In bell hooks (Ed.), *Teaching to transgress: Education as the practice of freedom* (pp. 59-75). New York: Routledge.

hooks, b. (1995). *Killing rage: Ending racism.* New York: Henry Holt and Company.

hooks, b. (1996). *Bone black: Memories of girlhood.* New York: Henry Holt and Company.

hooks, b. (2000). Revolutionary parenting. In b. hooks (Ed.) *Feminist theory: From margin to center* (2nd ed., pp. 133-147). Cambridge, MA: South End Press.

hooks, b. (2003). *Teaching community: A pedagogy of hope.* New York: Routledge.

hooks, b. (2007a). Revolutionary parenting. In A. O' Reilly (Ed.), *Maternal theory essential readings* (pp. 145-156). Toronto: Demeter Press.

hooks, b. (2007b). Homeplace: A site of resistance. In A. O' Reilly (Ed.), *Maternal theory essential readings* (pp. 266-273). Toronto: Demeter Press.

James, S. M. (1999). Mothering: A possible black feminist link to social transformation. In A. P. A. Busia, S. M. James & I. ebrary (Eds.), *Theorizing black feminisms: The visionary pragmatism of black women* (pp. 44-54). New York: Routledge.

Jenkins, N. L. (1998). Black women and the meaning of motherhood. In S. Abbey, & A. O'Reilly (Eds.), *Redefining motherhood: Changing identities and patterns* (pp. 201-213). Toronto: Sumach Press.

Jeckyl, W. (1966). *Jamaican song and story: Anancy stories, digging tunes, and ring tunes.* New York: Dover Publications.

Johal, G.S. (2005). Order in K.O.S. on race, rage and method. In G. J. S. Dei and G. S. Johal (Eds.), *Anti-racist research methodologies* (pp. 269-289). New York: Peter Lang.

Kiesinger, C. (1998). From interviewing to story: Writing Abbie's life. *Qualitative Inquiry,* 4, 71-95.

Kincaid, J. (1998). *A small space.* New York: Penguin.

Kincaid, J. (1985). *Annie John.* New York: Farrar, Straus and Giroux.

Kincaid, J. (1997). *The autobiography of my mother.* New York: Penguin.

Kincheloe, J. L., & Semali, L. (1999a). What is indigenous knowledge and why should we study it? In L. Semali, & J. L. Kincheloe (Eds.), *What is indigenous knowledge? : Voices from the academy* (pp. 3-58). New York: Falmer Press.

Kincheloe, J. L., & Semali, L. (Eds.) (1999b). *What is indigenous knowledge? : Voices from the academy.* New York: Falmer Press.

King, T. (2003). *The truth about stories: A native narrative.* Toronto: House of Anansi Press Inc.

Knowles, J. G. (1994). *Through preservice teachers' eyes.* New York: Merrill.

Knowles, J. G. (2001). Writing the professor: Thomas. In A. L. Cole & J. G. Knowles (Eds.) *Lives in Context* (pp. 230-232). Lanham, MD: Altamira Press.

Knowles, J. G., Luciani, T. C., Cole, A. L., & Neilson, L. (2004). (Eds.). *Provoked by art: Theorizing arts-informed research.* Halifax, N.S: Backalong Books.

Knowles, J. G., Luciani, T. C., Cole, A. L., & Neilson, L. (2007). (Eds.). *The art of visual inquiry.* Halifax: Backalong Books.

Knowles, J. G., & Promislow, S., (2008a). Using an arts methodology to create a thesis or dissertation. In A.L. Cole and J.G. Knowles (Eds.), *Handbook of the arts in qualitative research: Perspectives, methodologies, examples and issues* (pp. 511-523). Thousand Oaks, CA: Sage Publications.

Knowles, J. G., Promislow, S., & Cole, A.L., Eds. (2008b). *Creating scholartistry: Imagining the arts-informed thesis or dissertation.* Halifax: Backalong Books.

Kovach, M. (2009). *Indigenous methodologies: Characteristics, conversations and contexts.* Toronto: University of Toronto Press.

Lareau, A. (2003). *Unequal childhoods: Class, race, and family life.* Berkeley, CA: University of California Press.

Lattas, A. (1993). Essentialism, memory and resistance: Aboriginality and the politics of authenticity. *Oceana,* 63 (2), 240-267.

Lawson-Bush, V. (2004). How black mothers participate in the development of manhood and masculinity: What do we know about black mothers and their sons? *Journal of Negro Education,* 73(4), 381-391.

Lawson, E. (2000). Black women's mothering in a historical and contemporary perspective understanding the past, forging the future. *Journal of the Association for Research on Mothering*, 2(2), 22-30.

Lorde, A. (1997). The uses of anger: women responding to racism. In Bart Schneider (Ed.), *Race: An anthology in the first person* (pp. 99-109). New York: Three Rivers Press.

Lorde, A. (1997b). *Now that I am forever with child. The collected Poems of Audre Lorde.* New York: W.W Norton.

Lorde, A. (1982). *Zami: A new spelling of my name.* Berkeley, CA: Crossing Press.

Lorde, A. (2007). *Sister outsider: Essays and speeches by Audre Lorde.* Berkeley, CA: Crossing Press.

Lyle, E. (2009). A process of becoming: In favour of a reflexive narrative approach. *The Qualitative Report*, 14(2), 293-298.

Macedo, D. (1999). Decolonizing indigenous knowledge. In L. Semali, & J. L. Kincheloe (Eds.), *What is indigenous knowledge? Voices from the academy* (pp. xi-xvi). New York: Falmer Press.

Mackey, A. (2000). Return to the m(other) to heal the self: Identity, selfhood and community in toni morrison's beloved. *Journal of the Association for Research on Mothering*, 2(2), 42.

Magwaza, T. (2003). Perceptions and experiences of motherhood: A study of blackand white mothers of Durban, South Africa, *Jenda: A Journal of Culture and African Women Studies*. Available online http://www.jendajournal.com/jenda/issue4/magwaza. html. Accessed September 12, 2008.

Mahia, M. (1999). Indigenous knowledge and schooling: A continuum between conflict dialogue. In J. L. Kincheloe, & L. M. Semali (Eds.), *What is indigenous knowledge? voices from the academy* (pp. 59-77). New York: Falmer Press.

McLaughlin, T. & Tierney, W. (1993). *Naming silenced lives: Personal narratives and the process of educational change.* New York: Routledge.

Marshall, E. Z. (2001). 'The anansi syndrome': A debate concerning anansi's influence on Jamaican culture. *Journal of Postcolonial Writing*, 39(1), 127-136.

Marshall, E. Z. (2006) From messenger of the gods to muse of the people: The shifting contexts of anansi's metamorphosis.

Society for Caribbean Studies Annual Conference Papers, Vol.7. Available online at: www.caribbeanstudies.org.uk/papers/2006/olvol7p6.PDF. Accessed July 11, 2011.

Marshall, E. Z. (2007). Liminal spider: Symbol of order and chaos and exploration of anansi's roots amongst the asante of Ghana. *Caribbean Quarterly* 53(3), 30-40.

Marshall, E. Z. (2007) 'Tracking anansi'. *Caribbean Beat.* Available at: http://www.meppublishers.com/online/caribbean-beat/past_issues/index.php?pid=2000&id=cb88-1-47. Accessed July 11, 2011.

Mello, R. (2001). The power of storytelling: How oral narrative influences children's relationships in classrooms. *International journal of education and the arts,* 2(1). http://www.ijea.org/v2n1/. Accessed November 7, 2011.

Moen, T. (2006). Reflections of the narrative research approach. *International Journal of Qualitative Methods,* 5(4), 56-69.

Mogadime, D. (1998). A daughter's praise poem for her mother: Historicizing community activism and racial uplift among women." *Canadian Women's Studies/les cahiers de la femme,* 18(2/3), 86-91.

Mogadime, D. (2000). Black girls/black women centred texts and black teachers as othermothers. *Journal of the Association for Research on Mothering,* 2(2), 222-233.

Morrison, T. (1977). *Song of solomon* New York: New American Library.

Morrison, T. (1981). *Tar baby.* New York: Alfred A. Knopf.

Morrison, T. (1987). The site of memory. In W. Zinsser (Ed.) *Inventing the truth: The art and craft of memoir* (pp. 103-124). Boston: Houghton Miffin.

Morrison, T. (1998). *Playing in the dark: Whiteness and the literary imagination.* New York: Vintage Books.

Morrison, T. (2000). *The bluest eye.* New York: Alfred A. Knopf.

Morrison, T. & Moyers, B. D. Public Affairs Television (Firm). (2004). *Toni Morrison: A writer's work/a production of Public Affairs Television.* Princeton, NJ: Films for the Humanities and Sciences.

Nnaemeka, O. (1998). The politics of mothering. *Journal of Third World Studies,* 15(2), 195-199.

Nzegwu, N. (2005). The epistemological challenge of motherhood to patriliny. Jenda: *A Journal of Culture and African Women's Studies*, (5), Available from: http://www.jendajournal.com/issue5/nzegqu.htm. Accessed September 12, 2008.

Nzegwu, N. (2006). *Family matters: Feminist concepts in african philosophy of culture.* Albany, NY: State University of New York Press.

Oyewùmí, O. (2003b). Aiyammo: Theorizing african motherhood. *Jenda: A Journal of Culture and African Women's Studies*, (4). Available from: http:www.jendajournal.com/issue4/oyewumi. htm. Accessed September 12, 2008.

O'Reilly, A. (1998). Mothers, daughters, and feminism today: Empowerment, egency, narrative and motherline. *Canadian Woman's Studies/les cahiers de la femme*, 18(2,3), 16-21.

O'Reilly, A. (2000). 'I come from a line of uppity irate black women': African american feminism on motherhood, the motherline, and the mother-daughter relationship. In Andrea O'Reilly and Sharon Abbey (Eds.), *Mothers, daughters: Connection, empowerment, and transformation* (pp. 143-59). Lanham, MD: Rowman and Littlefield.

O'Reilly, A. (2004a). *Toni Morrison and motherhood: A politics of the heart.* Albany, NY: State University of New York Press.

O'Reilly, A. (2004b). *Mother outlaws: Theories and practices of empowered mothers.* Toronto: Demeter Press.

O'Reilly, A. (2004c). Introduction. In Andrea O'Reilly (Ed.), *From mothering to motherhood: The legacy of Adrienne Richs' of woman born* (pp. 1-23). Albany, NY: State University of New York Press.

O'Reilly, A. (2006). *Rocking the cradle: Thoughts on feminism, motherhood and the possibility of empowered mothering.* Toronto: Demeter Press.

O'Reilly, A. (2007a). Feminist Mothering. In A. O'Reilly (Ed.) *Maternal theory essential readings* (pp. 792-821). Toronto: Demeter Press.

O'Reilly, A. (2007b). *Maternal theory: Essential readings.* Toronto: Demeter Press.

O'Reilly, A.(2008). Introduction. In A. O'Reilly (Ed.) *Feminist mothering* (pp. 1-22).Toronto: Demeter Press.

O'Reilly, A., Ruddick, S. (2009a). A conversation about maternal thinking. In A. O'Reilly (Ed.) *Maternal thinking: Philosophy, politics, practice* (pp. 14-38).Toronto: Demeter Press.

O'Reilly, A. (2009b). Introduction. In A. O'Reilly (Ed.)*Maternal thinking: Philosophy, politics, practice* (pp. 1-13).Toronto: Demeter Press.

O'Reilly, A. (2010). *Encyclopedia of mothering*. New York: Sage Press.

Onuora, A. N. (2013). HERstory is OURstory: An Afro-indigenous response to the call for "truth" in narrative representation. *Cultural Studies <=> Critical Methodologies*, 13(5), 400-407.

Onuora, A. N. (2013). Killing me softly: On mother daughter resistance. *Canadian Woman Studies/les cahiers de la femme's* special issue on "Women Writing 4," 30 (1), 48-50.

Onuora, A. N. (2012). I feel therefore I can Be/long: Cultural bearing as maternal activism. *Journal of Motherhood Initiative for Research and Community Involvement*, (3.2), 206-212.

Pedraill, Z. S. (2007). A big boy/anancy tale: The trickster motif propelling a narrative of resistance in oliver senior's "Ascot." *Odesia*, 8, 173-186.

Patton, V. (2000). Policing our daughter's bodies: Mothering in african literature. *Journal of the Association for Research on Mothering*, 2(2), 176-187.

PerrymanMark, C. A. (2000). Resistance and surrender: Mothering young black and feminist. *Journal of the Association for Research on Mothering*, 2(2), 130-138.

Razack, S. (1993). Story telling for social change. *Gender and Education*, 5(1), 55-70.

Reynolds, J. D. (Ed.) (2006a). *Jabari: authentic jamaican dictionary of the jamic language featuring, Jamaican patwa and rasta iyaric, pronunciations and definitions*. Waterbury, CN: Around the Way Books.

Reynolds, J. D. (2006b). Who seh wi chat patwa (patois)? Available from: http://www.jamaicans.com/speakja/patoisarticle/ notpatoisbutjamic.shtml. Accessed July 11, 2011.

Rich, A. (1986). *Of woman born: Motherhood as experience and institution*.New York: W.W. Norton.

Rodriguez, D. (2006). Un/masking identity: Healing our wounded souls. *Qualitative Inquiry,* 12 (6), 1067-1090.

Rodriguez, D. (2009). The usual suspect: Negotiating white student resistance and teacher authority in a predominantly white classroom. *Cultural Studies/Critical Methodologies, 9,* 483-508.

Rodriguez, D. (2011). Silent rage and the politics of resistance: Countering seductions of whiteness and the road to politicization and empowerment. *Qualitative Inquiry,* 17 (7) 589-598.

Ruddick, S. (1989). *Maternal thinking: Toward a politic of peace.* Boston: Beacon Press.

Sbrocchi, S. (2008). Sketchy Lines. In J. G. Knowles, S. Promislow, & A. L. Cole (Eds.), *Creating scholartistry: Imagining the arts-informed thesis or dissertation* (pp. 198-206). Halifax: Backalong Books.

Smith, L. T. (1999). *Decolonizing methodologies: Research and indigenous peoples.* New York: St. Martin's Press.

Soloranzo, D. (1998). Critical race theory, race, gender micro-aggressions, and teh experience of Chicana and Chicano scholars. *Qualitative Studies in Education,* 11(1), 121-136.

Steele, C. P. (2000). Drawing strength from our mothers: Tapping the roots of black women's history. *Journal of the Association for Research on Mothering,* 2(2), 7-17.

Thomas, W. (2000). "You'll become a lioness": African-american women talk about mothering. *Journal of the Association for Research on Mothering,* 2(2), 52-65.

Tillmann-Healy, L. (1999). *Life projects: A narrative ethnography of gay-straight friendship.* Unpublished doctoral dissertation, University of South Florida.

Traore, A. (1979). Evolving relations between mothers and children in rural Africa. *International Social Science Journal,* 31(3), 486-491.

Ungar, M. (2011). The social worker—A novel: The advantages of fictional re-presentation of life narratives. *Cultural Studies/ Critical Methodologies,* 11(3), 290-302.

Villaverde, L. E. (2000). Border crossings: The act and implications in the production of art vis à vis patriarchy and whiteness. In N. M. Rodriguez & L. E. Villaverde (Eds.) *Dismantling white privilege: Pedagogy, politics, and whiteness* (pp. 41-58). New York: Peter Lang.

Walkerdine, V. & Lucy, H. (1989). *Democracy in the kitchen: Regulating mothers and socializing daughters.* Camden Town, London: Virago.

Wane, N. N. (2000a). Reflections on the mutuality of mothering: Women, children, and othermothering. *Journal of the Association for Research on Mothering*, 2 (2), 105-116.

Wane, N. (2000b). Indigenous knowledge: Lesson from the elders-a Kenyan case study. In G. J. S. Dei, B. L. Hall & D. G. Rosenberg (Eds.), *Indigenous knowledges in global contexts: Multiple readings of our world* (pp. 54-69). Toronto: OISE/UT book published in association with University of Toronto Press.

Willey, N. (2000). Ibuza vs. lagos: The feminist traditional buchi emecheta. *Journal of the Association for Research on Mothering*, 2(2), 155-166.

Wilson, S. (2007). What is an indigenist research paradigm? *Canadian Journal of Native Education*, 30(2), 193-195.

Williams, P. (1991). *The alchemy of race and rights.* Cambridge, MA: Harvard University Press.

Wing, A. (1997). *Critical race feminism.* New York: New York University Press.